BAKUMATSU JAPAN

Published by TOYO PRess:

TOYO REFERENCE SERIES
Isabella Lucy Bird, *Traveling Japan's Deep Interior*
John la Farge, *An Artist in Japan*
Vasilii Golovnin, *Captive in Japan*
Lafcadio Hearn, *Hearn's Japan. Vols. I-XIV*
Lucian Swift Kirtland, *Samurai Trails*
Ernest Satow, *Japan's Critical Years*
Marie Stopes, *A Japanese Journal*

TOYO ILLUSTRATED EDITIONS
Eiko Ozaki, *Warriors of Old Japan*
Lafcadio Hearn, *Hearn's Japan*

BAKUMATSU JAPAN

Travels through a Vanishing World

AIMÉ HUMBERT

EDITED BY WILLIAM DE LANGE

TOYO REFERENCE SERIES

First edition, 2019

Originally published as *Japan and the Japanese*

Published by TOYO Press

ISBN 978-94-92722-201

Contents

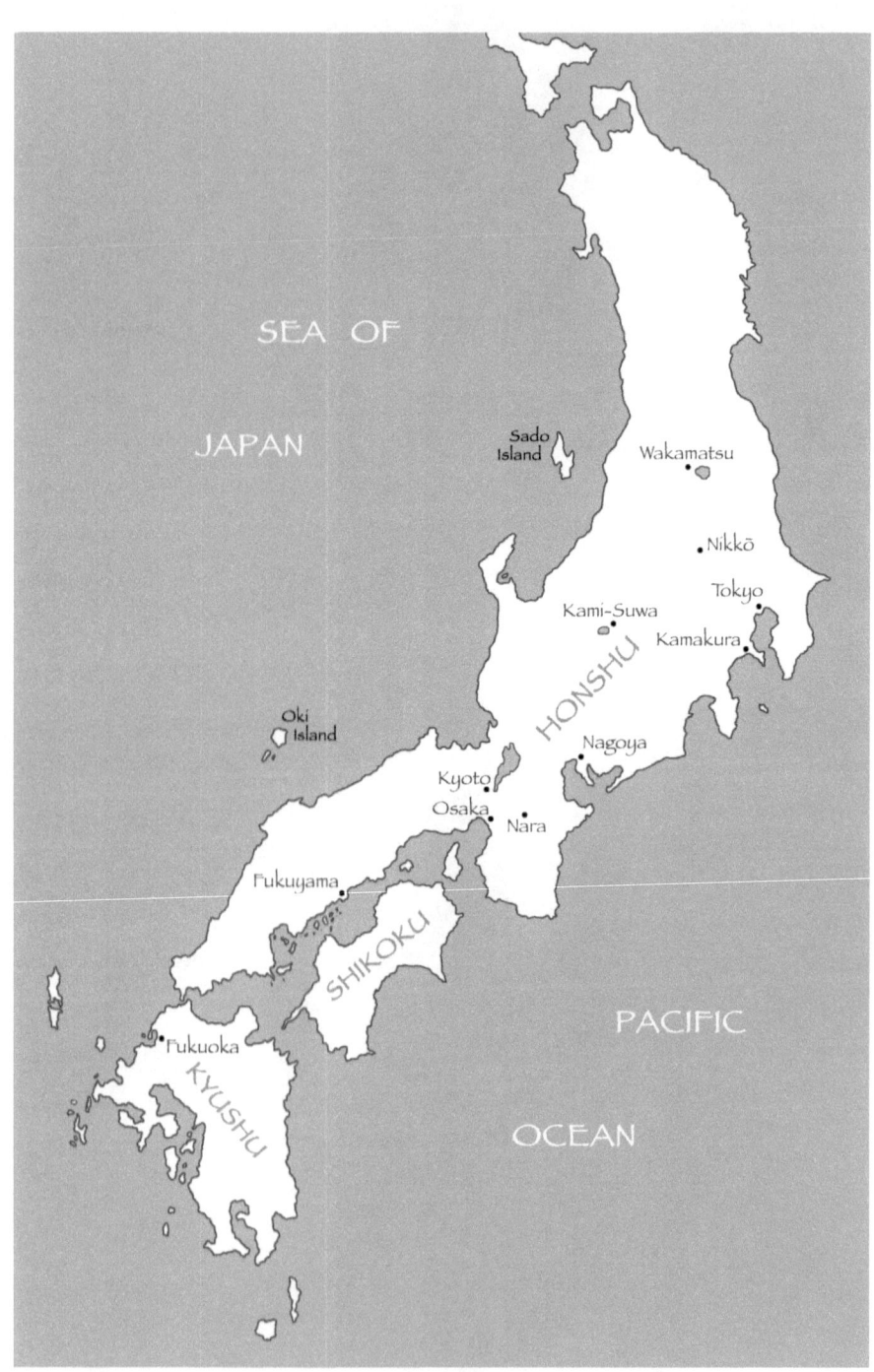

SEA OF

JAPAN

Sado
Island

Wakamatsu

Nikkō

Tokyo

Kami-Suwa

Kamakura

HONSHU

Oki
Island

Nagoya

Kyoto

Osaka

Nara

Fukuyama

SHIKOKU

PACIFIC

Fukuoka

KYUSHU

OCEAN

Inland Sea

The Inland Sea of Japan is bounded by the southern coasts of Honshu, and the northern coasts of Kyushu, and Shikoku. It is more like a canal than a real mediterranean sea, being a communication established, at the height of the thirty-fourth degree of north latitude, between the Sea of Japan, or, more strictly, of the Tsushima Straits, on the western coast of Honshu, and the Pacific Ocean, which washes the southern and eastern shores of the same archipelago. The whole of the Japanese Mediterranean is sometimes known as the Sea of Suo, or Suo-*nada*. Each of the provinces by which it is surrounded contains one or several *han*, or lordships, belonging to feudal princes, *daimyō*, who enjoy considerable independence, and generally derive large revenues from their estates. Among others, the family of the *daimyō* of Kyushu may be mentioned, as drawing from their patrimonial domains an annual revenue equivalent to the sum of £352,000, the *daimyō* of Aki, whose revenue is £279,400, the *daimyō* of Nagato, whose fortune amounts to £230,160. And the *daimyō* of Bizen, who draws £198,400. The Japanese Mediterranean, like the European sea so called, is divided into several basins. They are five in number, and are named from the most important of the provinces that overlook them, so that the Inland Sea bears five different names throughout its longitudinal course from west to east.

In the midst of the natural wealth that surrounds them, the large, industrious, and intelligent population of the country parts of Japan have for their entire possessions only a humble shed, a few working implements, some pieces of cotton cloth, a few mats, a cloak of straw, a little store of tea, oil, rice, and salt, for furniture, nothing but two or three cooking utensils—

in a word, only the strict necessaries of existence. All the remaining product of their labour belongs to the owners of the soil, the feudal lords.

The absence of a middle class gives a miserable aspect to the Japanese villages. Liberal civilization would have covered the borders of the Inland Sea with pretty hamlets and elegant villas. The uniformity of the rustic dwellings is broken by temples, but they are to be distinguished at a distance only by the vast dimensions of their roofs, and by the imposing effect of the ancient trees that are almost always to be found in their vicinity. Buddhist pagodas, which are lofty towers with pointed roofs, adorned with galleries on each floor, are much leas common in Japan than in China.

On entering the basin of Hyōgo, we came in sight of a town of some importance, on the coast of Shikoku. It is called Imabari. A vast sandy beach, rarely to be found in Japan, stretched back to a kind of suburb, in which we could discern a busy concourse of people, apparently carrying on market business. Above the strand were fertile plains, whose undulating lines were lost in the mist at the foot of a chain of mountains bathed in sunshine. The principal peaks of this chain are from 1,000 to 1,600 yards in height.

Fortifications, or rather mounds of earth, behind which shone several banners, protected the batteries posted in front of the port. Some soldiers, standing in a group on the shore, followed our corvette with their eyes. There was nothing remarkable in the aspect of the town, except the sacred places, adorned by gigantic trees. Some time afterwards we passed, within rifle-range, a large Japanese steamer. Our pilot, whom we consulted, and who judged from the colors of the flag, informed us it was the property of the *daimyō* of Tosa. His estates are situated in the southern portion of the island of Shikoku, and they bring him in a very large annual revenue.

Most probably he was returning from a conference of the feudal party held in the city of Kyoto, at the court of the hereditary emperor of Japan, and had embarked at Kobe, in order to regain his own province by the Bungo canal. What were his sentiments on beholding a strange corvette cleaving the waters of the Inland Sea? Does he flatter himself that he can repel the civilization of the West by the arms it places at his disposal? Does he know where steam will lead him?

Counting up all the war steamers which, to our knowledge, have been furnished to Japan by Europe and America, we make the number fourteen.

The first, the yacht *Solenburg*, was given to the *shōgun* by the King of the Netherlands, another, the yacht *Emperor*, by the Queen of England, the others have been sold by the governments or the traders of the West, either to the *shōgun*, or to certain of the principal *daimyō*, such as of Mito, Nagato, Satsuma, and Tosa.

A little before sunset we saw, on the coast of Shikoku, a feudal castle, remarkable for its picturesque site on the summit and the sides of a wooded hill, at whose feet a rustic hamlet seemed to shelter itself under the protection of the ancient lordly towers. It is the castle of Marugame, the residence of *daimyō* Kyōgoku Akiyuki, whose revenues are valued at £40,000.

The castles of the *daimyō* are generally at a distance from the towns and villages. They are composed, in most instances, of a vast quadrangular enclosure, within thick and lofty crenellated walls, surrounded by a moat, and flanked at the corners, or surmounted at intervals throughout their extent, by small square towers with slightly sloping roofs. In the interior are the park, the gardens, and the actual residence of the *daimyō*, comprising a main dwelling, and numerous dependencies. Sometimes a solitary tower, of a shape similar to the other buildings, rises in the middle of the feudal domain, and rears itself three or four stories higher than the external wall. As in the case of the Chinese pagodas, each story is surrounded by a roof, which but seldom supports a gallery. All the masonry is rough, and joined by cement, the woodwork is painted red and black, and picked out with copper ornaments, which are sometimes polished, but sometimes laden with verdigris. The tiles of the roof are slate-color. In general, richness of detail is less aimed at than the general effect resulting from the grandeur and harmony of the proportions of the buildings. In this respect, some of the seignorial residences of Japan deserve to figure among the remarkable architectural monuments of the peoples of Eastern Asia.

We anchored in a bay of the island of Shōdo, at the southern point of the province of Bitchū, and at the entrance of the basin of Arima. We were surrounded by mountains, at whose feet twinkled many lights shining in from houses. The stillness was unbroken, save by the distant barking of dogs. Next morning, April 24, very early, we were ploughing the peaceful waters of the Arima Basin. This basin is completely closed on the east by a single island, which divides it from the Izumi-*nada* (Osaka Bay) by a length of thirty miles. It is in the form of a triangle, whose apex, turned towards the north, faces the province of Arima, on the island of Honshu. This is the beautiful island of Awaji, which was the dwellingplace of the gods, and the cradle of the national mythology of the Japanese. The lowlands at its southern extremity are covered with a luxuriant vegetation, and the soil rises gently into cultivated or wooded hills until they touch the boundaries of a chain of mountains from 300 to 700 yards in height. Awaji belongs to the *daimyō* of Awa, whose annual revenue amounts to £60,000. It is separated from the island of Shikoku by the passage of Naruto on the west, and from the island of Honshu by the Strait of Akashi on the north, and the Strait of Kitan on the east.

The greater number of the steamers which cross the Japanese Mediterranean from west to east, pass from the basin of Arima into that of Izumi, where they generally touch at the important commercial town of Kobe. And from there they enter the Pacific Ocean by the Strait of Kitan. That passage of Naruto, which leads directly from the basin of Arima into the Pacific Ocean, is shorter than the former, but much less frequented because it is considered a dangerous channel for high-decked vessels.

We saw the coasts drawing nearer and nearer to us, as we descended, towards the south-west corner of this triangular piece of land. At the same time a promontory of the island of Shikoku rose above the horizon on our right, and seemed to stretch continuously onward in the direction of Awaji. Very soon we found ourselves in a passage from whence we could distinctly see the beautiful vegetation of the coast of Shikoku and the coast of Awaji. At length we saw the gates of the strait. On the left, rocks surmounted by pines, forming the front of the island of Awaji; on the right, a solitary rock, or islet, also bearing a few pines, forming the front of the island of Shikoku. Between them the sea, like a bar of breakers, though the weather was calm, afar, the undulating ocean, without a speck of foam, the tossing of the waves in the passage being solely the result of the violence of the current. All around us, on the waves and at the foot of the rocks, were thousands of seabirds, screaming, fluttering, and diving for the prey which the sea, stirred to its depths by the current, was perpetually tossing up to them. Several fishing boats were out, not on the canal—that would have been impossible—but behind the rocks, in the creeks of the little solitary islet and of Shikoku.

4

Below Awaji, the united waters of the two straits of Naruto and Kitan pour into Wakayama Bay, which washes the shores of the province of Awa, on Shikoku, and of the province of Kii, on Honshu. We sailed for some time yet in sight of the latter. Then the land disappeared from our eyes, and we soon perceived, by the wide-rolling motion of the waves, that we were on the outer sea, in the immense domain of the Pacific Ocean.

I occupied myself, during the whole evening, in recalling the recollections of my journey. And I could find nothing out of Switzerland to compare with the effect of the beautiful Japanese scenery. Since then, several Japanese, travelling in Switzerland, have told me that no other country awakened so vividly the remembrance of their own. Still more frequently I transported myself in fancy to one or other of the archipelagoes of the Inland Sea, earnestly desiring the advent of that hour when the breath of liberty will give them, in the Far East, the importance which formerly belonged, in Europe, to the archipelago of our Mediterranean.

They cannot be blended into a general impression. Nothing is less uniform than the scenery of the shores of the Inland Sea. It is a series of pictures that vary infinitely, according to the greater or lesser proximity of the coasts, or to the aspect of the islands on the horizon. There are grand marine scenes, where the lines of the sea blend with sandy beaches sleeping under the golden rays of the sun, while in the distance, the misty mountains form a dim background. There are little landscapes, very clear, trim, and modest, a village at the back of a peaceful bay, surrounded by green fields, over which towers a forest of pines, just as one may see by a lake in the Jura on a fine morning in June.

Sometimes, when the basins grew narrow, and the islands in front seemed to shut us in, I remembered the Rhine above Boppard. Yet the Japanese scenery is more calm and bright than the romantic landscapes to which I allude. The abrupt slopes, the great masses of shade, the shifting lines, are replaced by horizontal levels, by a beach, a port, and terraces, in the distance are rounded islands, sloping hills, conical mountains. These pictures have their charms, the imagination, no less than the eye, rests in the contemplation of them. But it would seek in vain that melancholy attraction that, according to the notions of European taste, seems inseparable from the enjoyment.

Laying aside the question of the picturesque, which is not the essential element of our relations with the Far East, I hope that, sooner or later, a chain of Western colonies will be formed at Japan, peacefully developing the natural and commercial resources of that admirable country, along a line marked by Yokohama, Kobe, Shimonoseki, and Nagasaki. It might have a regular service of steamers. The trading steamers of America, as well as those of China, might maintain the relations of the two worlds with the king of the archipelagoes of the Pacific. Europeans, weary of the tropical climate or the burthen of business in China, might seek pure and strengthening air, and pass some weeks of repose on the shores of the Japanese Mediterranean. How many families settled in China, how many wives and children of Europeans, would be delighted to profit, during the trying summer months, by this refuge, as beautiful and salubrious as Italy, and yet near their actual home!

But while imagination, forestalling the march of time and the triumphs of civilization, evokes the charms of a European society from the bosom of the isles of the Inland Sea, or Suo-*nada*, I must acknowledge that I privately congratulated myself on having seen the Japanese Mediterranean in its primitive condition, while one may still discover something, and has to ask the pilots the names of the islands, the mountains, and the villages, and to cast anchor for the night in some creek called "fair port" by the natives.

On the night of April 24, after having doubled the southern point of the great island of Honshu; i.e., the promontory of Izumo (Cape Shionomisaki), situated at the southern extremity of the principality of Kii, we sailed, during the whole day on the 25th, with the current which the Japanese call Kuroshio, which runs from south-west to north-east, at the rate of from thirty-five to forty miles a day. It is a current of hot water, whose maximum temperature is 30° Centigrade.

The weather was fine, and the sea a shining emerald-green. I passed many hours on the poop, in stillness and vague contemplation. For the first time I enjoyed the pleasure of sailing. The silence that reigned on board added to the majestic effect of the ship, laden up to the summit of her masts with her triple wings of white. It was as though the fires had been extinguished, and the noise of the engines hushed, that we might present ourselves more respectfully at the gates of the residence of the *shōgun*. But when night fell, the fires were lighted again, in case of accident, for the land winds frequently cause much trouble to the ships in the Bay of Edo. On the 26th, at daybreak, we came within sight of six small mountainous islands, which looked like signals set up at the entrance of this vast arm of the sea.

The sun rose, and presented, amid the salt sea mists of the horizon, that image of a scarlet globe that forms the national arms of Japan. His earliest rays lighted up Cape Irozaki, on the Izu Peninsula, whilst ahead of us, in the east, we beheld the smoke of the two craters of Ōshima Island. At the head of a bay in the Izu Peninsula is situated the town of Shimoda, the first, but the least important of the commercial places to which we come when sailing up Edo Bay. The Americans obtained an authorization to found an establishment there in 1854. Some time afterwards the harbour of Shimoda was destroyed by an earthquake, and no mention was made of that place in the treaties of 1858.

A number of fishing boats are to be seen on the coast, and several three-masted vessels are going to the mainland of Honshu and the surrounding islands. The scene is full of life, and sparkling with brilliant and harmonious color, the wide sky is a splendid azure, the pale green sea has no longer the sombre hues of the great deeps, but shines with the limpid brightness that characterizes it on the rocky coasts of Japan. The isles are decked in the brilliant foliage of the spring, the harsh brown of the rocks is streaked with shades of ochre. And the white sails of the native barques, the snow crests of Miyake-shima, and the smoke from the craters of Ōshima, complete the beautiful marine scene.

Having reached Missisipy Bay[1] we made out, for the first time, the summit of Fuji-*yama*, the "Matchless Mountain," an extinct volcano 12,450 feet above the level of the sea. It is fifty nautical miles from the coast, on the west of the bay, and except for the chain of the mountains at its base, completely isolated. The effect of this immense solitary pyramid, covered with eternal snow, surpasses description. It lends inexpressible solemnity to the scenery of Edo Bay, already more sombre than that of the bay, by reason of the closer proximity of the shores, the somewhat sandy hue of the seawater, and the immense quantity of cedars, pines, and other dark-foliaged trees which crown the crests of all the hills along the coast.

1 Missisippi Bay has been largely reclaimed.

At length we double Point Treaty,[2] a picturesque promontory where the convention between Commodore Matthew Calbraith Perry and the commissioners of the *shōgun* was signed. And all of a sudden, behind this promontory, we see the quays and the city of Yokohama stretching along a marshy beach, bounded on the south and west by a ring of wooded hills. A score of ships of war, and merchant vessels, English, Dutch, French, and American, are lying out in the roads, almost opposite the foreign quarter, which may easily be recognized by its white houses and its consular flags. Native junks are lying at anchor at some distance from the jetties of the port and the store houses of the custom house. We pass by these slowly, and steam at half speed in front of the Japanese city, in which all the houses, except a certain number of shops, are built of wood, and seem to have only one storey above the ground floor.

When we had come opposite to the Benten-dōri, the quarter situated at the extremity of the beach of Yokohama, and at the mouth of a wide river, our corvette anchored, near the Dutch legation, which was at that time the only European residence in that part of Yokohama.

2 Treaty Point is now the western landing point of the Tokyo Bay Aqua Line.

Yokohama

That portion of the Japanese city of Yokohama called Benten-dōri derives its name from a sea goddess, who is worshipped in an island situated to the north-west of our residence. Before the arrival of the Europeans, this sacred place was surrounded only by a small town, in which dwelt fishermen and farmers, separated by a swamp from the not less modest little town of Yokohama. Now, quays, streets, modern buildings, have invaded the entire space that extends from the promontory of Treaty Point to the river, from which we are divided only by a range of Japanese barracks and a guard house.

Among the streets that extend to the seabeach from Benten-dōri, there is one shaded by a plantation of firs. On passing through the municipal barrier which the police keep open during the day and shut at night, the stranger finds himself in front of a long avenue of fir trees, headed by a sacred gate called a *torii*. It is composed of two pillars slightly inclined towards each other, so that they meet at last at an acute angle, if at a certain elevation their pyramidal development were not checked. And joined by two horizontal transverse beams, of which the uppermost is the thicker, and is curved upwards at both ends. The *torii* invariably announces the vicinity of a temple, a shrine, or a sacred place of some sort. A grotto, a waterfall, a gigantic tree, a fantastic rock, all things which we prosaically call natural curiosities, the Japanese regards with pious veneration or with superstitious fear, according to whether they are more or less governed by the Buddhist demonology. The monks of the country never fail to give tangible form to this popular tendency by erecting a *torii* close to each remarkable place.

The pine trees along the Benten avenue are lofty, slender, and for the most part bent by the continuous action of the sea breezes. At regular distances long poles are nailed on them crosswise, on which, on festival days, the monks hang inscriptions, wreaths, and swinging banners.

The avenue ends in a second *torii*, which, with due regard to perspective, is not so lofty as the first. On approaching it, one is surprised to find that the avenue makes a sudden bend and prolongs itself on the right. Here all is mystery, a waste ground, covered with rank grasses, bushes, and slender pines with aerial foliage. On the left is the calm transparent water of a little bay formed by an arm of the river. In front is a wooden bridge, built in a style of severe elegance, wide, and excessively curved. Behind this bridge is a third *torii*, thrown out against the thick foliage of a grove of fine trees. The whole forms a strange picture, with something in it that excite a secret apprehension. This bridge, whose pillars are decorated with ornaments in copper, finally admits us to the sacred place. The third *torii*, bearing on its summit an inscription in gold letters on a black ground, is entirely built of fine granite of remarkable whiteness. And the tombs, which are tastefully disposed on the left side of the avenue, are constructed of the same material.

The Benten shrine, almost entirely hidden by the branches of the cedars and pines which surround it, faces us. But the mysterious gloom hardly permits us to discern the flight of steps on which the people kneel who come to worship before the altar of the goddess. Should the shrine be empty, one of the monks in attendance may be summoned by shaking a long strip of woollen material that hangs beside the entrance, with a bunch of pebbles attached to it. The monk comes out of his retreat immediately, and proceeds, according to the requirements of the visitor, to give him advice, to distribute tapers or amulets, to undertake to recite prayers, in fact to perform any of the ceremonies of their worship—of course for the consideration of a fee.

As a Japanese, before he presents himself at the sanctuary, must wash and dry his hands and face, in a small chappell, at some distance from the shrine, on the right, is a basin containing the holy water intended for ablutions, and napkins of silk crape suspended on a roller, like the hand-towels in a sacristy. One of two chapels close by contains the big drum that serves the purpose of a bell for the shrine, the other the ex-voto offerings of the faithful. The priests who serve the shrine of Benten do not appear to live in opulence. Their attire is generally dirty and neglected. And the expression of their faces is sullen and malevolent towards strangers, who are glad to keep at a respectful distance from these holy persons.

I had only one opportunity of seeing them officiate, it was on the occasion of a procession on their local festival day. On ordinary days, it appears that they merely give audiences. I have rarely seen men resort to their ministrations. Their habitual clients are peasant women, fishermen, and casual pilgrims. I have frequently heard, at sunset, the beating of *taiko*, which, except at great solemnities, form the whole orchestra of the shrine of Benten. The monks perform interminable music on this monstrous instrument, always in the same rhythm, four equal loud notes, followed by four equal deep notes, and so on, for hours on end, probably the length of time required to drive away the evil influences. Nothing can exceed the melancholy impression produced by this deep-sounding noise, when, in the silence of the night, it blends with the sighing of the great cedar trees and the booming of the sea. It oppresses one like a nightmare. But indeed it may be said that the religion that finds expression in such customs weighs on the mind of the people like a dream, full of uneasiness and vague terror.

The obligatory accompaniment of the Japanese temples are teahouses, or restaurants, at which tea is principally supplied, but where *sake*, a fermented and highly intoxicating drink, may be had. The eatables are fruits, fish, rice, or wheaten cakes. And everyone smokes. The pipes are metal, the tobacco is very finely cut, and free from all narcotic admixture, opium-smoking is unknown in Japan. These establishments, where women are the attendants, and where external propriety is strictly observed, are, for the most part, places of ill fame. This is especially the case in respect to those situated in the vicinity of the *torii* at the shrine of Benten, a circumstance that probably dates from a period at which the little island dedicated to the patroness of the sea still attracted a considerable number of pilgrims. At present the altar of the goddess is singularly neglected. But there is a great military station in the neighborhood, with which the rule of the *shōgun*— that of the sword—has endowed the city of Yokohama. It occupies the entire space between the island of Benten and our dwelling.

The quarter of the *yakunin* is composed of the residences of government officers employed in the customs of the harbour police and that of other public places, of the military instruction, of the guard of the Japanese city, and the superintendents of the "free quarter."

The *yakunin* have no outward and visible sign of their functions except a large pointed hat of lacquered pasteboard, and two swords passed through the girdle on the left side, one of these is large and held with two hands, the other, a kind of blade intended for single combat, is small. These are the only warlike points in the equipment of these functionaries. They number several hundreds, they are almost all married, each has his separate lodging, and all seem to be placed on a footing of equality in this respect. It is not uninteresting to study the means the government of the *shōgun* has adopted for organizing this army of functionaries into a kind of camp, while retaining their domestic surroundings. This has been effected to a certain extent by the application of the cellular system to family life.

Picture a collection of wooden buildings, forming a long square, a lofty wooden wall towards the street, low doors at regular intervals, each giving access to a court, which contains a small garden, a water cistern, a kitchen, and other offices. Across the yard, on the ground floor, lies a spacious cell, which may be subdivided into two or three rooms by means of sliding partitions, the court and the cell comprise the lodging of a *yakunin* family. Each of the long blocks of which the streets in this quarter arc composed encloses at least a dozen of these dwellings, six ranged side by side, and then six back to back with the others. The cells arc all roofed with green tiles, and no roof is more lofty than another.

The *yakunin* quarter is a triumph of straight lines and uniformity. The streets are generally empty, because the men pass the greater part of the clay at the custom house or the guard houses. During the absence of its head, every family keeps itself within its narrow enclosure. Even the door, which is so low that one must stoop to pass through, is generally shut during this time of seclusion. This custom is, in one way, analogous to the precaution with which Turkish jealousy surrounds women. It arises from the position Japanese habits assign to the fathers of families. In each, his wife beholds her lord and master. In his presence she attends to her domestic duties with perfect ease and simplicity, caring nothing for the presence of a stranger.

In his absence she observes an extreme reserve, which we might be tempted to attribute to modesty, but which is more truthfully explained by the dependence and intimidation imposed on her by marriage.

By degrees neighborly relations were established between our residence and the *yakunin* quarter. In Japan, as elsewhere, small presents encourage friendship. We sent some white sugar and some Java coffee to certain families where we learned there were sick persons, or women in childbed, and these small offerings were gratefully received.

One day, when I was alone in the house, between four and five o'clock in the afternoon, the guard came to announce the arrival of a feminine deputation from the *yakunin* quarter, and to ask me whether he should send them away. These ladies had been authorized by their husbands to make their acknowledgments in person, but they had profited by the opportunity to express their wish to examine our European furniture. I told the porter that I would gladly undertake to do the honorus of the house to them. Presently I heard the clicking of a number of wooden shoes on the gravel walk in the garden, and, looking towards the foot of the verandah staircase in front of the room, I saw a group of smiling faces, among which I distinguished four married women, two young girls, and several children of all ages. The former were remarkable for the plainness of their dress, no ornament in the hair, no light materials or bright colors in their garments, no paint on their faces, but their teeth painted as black as ebony, as is becoming to all married women, according to Japanese ideas. The young girls, on the contrary, show off the natural whiteness of their teeth by a layer of carmine on their lips, put rouge on their cheeks, braid their thick hair with strips of scarlet crape, and wear wide girdles of many colors. The children's dress is simply a plain garment and a striped sash, they never wear any headdress, and their heads are shaven, except a few locks, some hanging loose, others tied together and arranged as a chignon.

After the customary salutations, the orators of the deputation—for three or four always spoke simultaneously—said many pretty things to me in Japanese, to which I replied in French, while I made signs to the company to enter the drawing room. It was quite clear they had understood me, I could not mistake the expression of thanks. And yet, instead of ascending the staircase, they seemed to be asking me for an explanation of some sort. At length my fair friends perceived my embarrassment, and, by adding gestures to language, asked me, "Ought we to take off our shoes in the garden, or will it suffice if we take them off in the verandah? "I pronounced in favor of the latter alternative, and my guests immediately ascended the stairs, removed their shoes and placed them in a line on the floor, and then gleefully trod the carpets of the drawing room—the children with bare feet, the grown-up persons in socks made of cotton cloth, divided into two unequal compartments, one for the great toe, and the other for the rest of the foot.

Their first impression was innocent admiration, to which general laughter succeeded when they all found themselves reflected at full length and on all sides, in the long mirrors that came down to the floor. While the younger members of the party indulged themselves in unwearied contemplation of a scene at once so novel and so attractive, the matrons asked me the meaning of the pictures adorning the room. I explained that they represented the King of Holland and his wife, and also several great princes of the reigning family. They bowed respectfully, but one of them, whose curiosity was not satisfied, said, timidly, that she supposed they had also taken the portrait of his Dutch majesty's groom? I took care not to undeceive her, because she would not have understood that it could be correct to represent a prince standing beside his saddle-horse and holding it by the bridle. Others, having attentively examined the velvet sofas and armchairs, told me how a dispute had arisen between them respecting the use of those articles of furniture. They agreed as to the easy chairs, it was, no doubt, intended that they should be sat on—but the sofas? Surely one ought to squat on them with crossed legs, especially when eating at the table in front of them. They sincerely pitied the gentlemen and ladies of the West, condemned to make such inconvenient use of these articles, and actually to sit with their legs hanging down.

My room, being open and on the same level, was speedily invaded, and almost everything in it was a subject of astonishment to my visitors, who were nonetheless daughters of Eve because they were born in Japan. They were particularly delighted with a set of uniform buttons bearing the Swiss federal cross, according to the military rule of my country. I had to give them some of these buttons, though I could not imagine to what use they could possibly apply them, since all Japanese garments, for the use of both sexes, are simply fastened by silken strings. The gift of a few articles of Parisian perfumery was highly appreciated, but I praised Eau de Cologne quite unsuccessfully. Cambric handkerchiefs are unknown in Japan. I showed them some specimens, very prettily embroidered by the clever needlewomen of Appenzell. But they explained to me that, though the *élégantes* of Edo might perhaps use them as cuffs for their wide and flowing robes, not the lowest woman of the people would hold in her hand or carry in her pocket a piece of material in which she blows her nose. There is, therefore, no chance at present that the little squares of paper, made from vegetable substances, which they carry in a fold of the dress, in the breast, or in a pocket in the sleeve, and which are thrown away as each is successively used, will be supplanted by our barbarous method. Eau de Cologne, however, might be used with advantage, to counteract the briny flavor of the well-water which is drunk at Benten.

Another point on which my visitors seemed to regard the superiority of Japanese civilization as incontestable, is their method of writing. The Japanese uses a brush, a stick of Chinese ink, and a roll of paper made from mulberry leaves. He carries those things about with him everywhere, the roll of paper is placed in his breast, the brush and the inkstand hang in a case from his girdle, together with his pipe and his tobaccobag.

In order to regain my advantage, I exhibited a case containing an assortment of sewing cotton, needles, and pins, and begged the lady *yakunin* to use them. They unanimously acknowledged the imperfection of the working materials of their country, where the sewing machine is unknown. Needlework does not occupy in Japan any place like that which it takes in our middle-class households, it is never produced during the long gossipping visits which the Japanese women interchange.

As in Europe men have recourse to the cigar, so in Japan they season their conversation with pipes.

The visit ended by my giving the children some prints representing Swiss landscapes and costumes, and showing their elders a photographic album containing likenesses of all the members of my family, which they examined with more than interest, with really touching emotion. It is within the domain of the natural affections that the unity, the identity of the human race, in every clime and among every people, makes itself most sensibly felt. What signifies diversity of idiom in the presence of that universal language which translates itself by the expression of the eye, by a tear on the eyelid, by sweet and touching intonations of the voice, like Mendelssohn's *Songs without Words*? The traveller is, in the sight of all primitive peoples, a being who deserves the deepest pity, for he is separated from all that constitutes the charm of life—the family, the paternal roof, the country of his ancestors. Religious admiration would be mingled with the compassion he inspires if he had left his country to accomplish a pious pilgrimage in a distant land, but that a man should cross the seas merely in the interest of terrestrial objects is a thing incomprehensible to the Japanese. They might admit the notion of my being a political exile, the victim of the severity of my government. But when they learn that I am neither a pilgrim nor proscribed, astonishment mingled with a kind of fright is added to their artless sympathy.

Truly, I am very far from Europe, in a world quite foreign to its civilization, and it was time that the West should come to these insular people, to teach them modes of thought and perception less incompatible with the genius of "business."

The Countrytside

All the good people who compose the population of the beach accost me in the friendliest manner. The children bring me beautiful glistening shells, and the women do their best to make me understand the culinary properties of the hideous little marine monsters which they pile up in their baskets. This spontaneous kindness and cordiality is a characteristic common to all the lower classes of Japanese society. More than once when I have been going on foot about the suburbs of Nagasaki or Yokohama, the country people have invited me to step inside their little enclosures. Then they would show me their flowers, and cut the best among them to make up a bouquet for me. It was always in vain that I offered them money, they never accepted it, and were not satisfied until I had crossed their threshold and partaken of tea and rice cakes with them. Spring is the most tempting season for exploring the coasts of Edo Bay. From the heights on its borders, the inland scene, stretching away to the foot of Fuji-*yama*, presents an uninterrupted succession of wooded hills and cultivated valleys, diversified by rivers or bays, which at a distance look like lakes. The villages on their banks are half hidden in rich foliage. And large farms, approached by shady roads, may be traced out at various points of the landscape.

The precocity of the vegetation in the rice grounds and on the cultivated hills, the quantity of evergreen trees on every side, deprives the springtide in Japan of that fresh and budding aspect which is one of its chief beauties elsewhere. And yet, where can there be found a more luxuriant spring vegetation, more rich in beautiful details! All along the hedges, in the orchards, and about the villages, tufts of flowers and foliage of dazzling hue stand out against the dark tints of a background of pines, firs, cedars, cypress, laurels, green oak, and bamboos. Here, we find the great white flowers of the wild mulberry, there, camellias growing in the open country, as tall as our apple-trees, everywhere, cherry trees, plum trees, peach trees, generally laden with double flowers, some quite white, others bright red, and sometimes white and red on the same branches, for many of the Japanese do not care at all for the fruit of these trees, but cultivate and graft them merely for the sake of the double flowers, and to vary or combine the species. The bamboo, much employed in the capacity of a support to these trees, frequently lends his elegant foliage to the branches of young fruit trees which have no other adornment than their bunches of flowers. But I love the bamboo most when it grows in solitary groups, like a tuft of gigantic reeds. There is nothing more picturesque in the whole landscape than these tall green polished stems, with their golden streaks and their tufted tops, and all around the chiefs the young slender offshoots with their feathered heads, and a multitude of long leaves streaming in the wind like thousands of fluttering pennons. The bamboo groves are fautorite subjects of study with the Japanese painters, whether they limit themselves to reproduce the graceful lines and harmonious effects, or enliven the picture by adding some of the live creatures which seek their verdant shelter—the little birds, the butterflies, and, in lonely places, the weasel, the ferret, the black squirrel, and the red-faced brown monkey.

All the waysides are bordered with violets, but they are scentless. The country produces a very small number of odoriferous plants, and it is remarkable that the lark, the nightingale, and other songbirds are very rare. Perhaps the lack of perfume and of song, in the midst of all the wealth of a luxuriant vegetation, helps to diminish the effect on the imagination the Japanese scenery ought to produce. It is certain that in contemplating it one does not experience that sense of dreamy exaltation and tenderness produced by the sight of a European landscape in the springtime, when nature is waking up. Without going into the question of the extent to which our sensibility is fed by the remembrances of childhood, and the traditional ideas thart find no application in the world of the Far East, I think the cooling of our enthusiasm may be accounted for by the fact that, in Japan, nature is over-cultivated.

With the exception of the forests and other plantations of trees, which the government maintain with praiseworthy care, the entire soil is invaded by cultivation to an extent that almost defies description. Early in April the fields outside the woods are covered with buckwheat in full flower. In four or five weeks' time, on the lower ground, they will be reaping the barley and wheat sown in November. In Japan they sow corn as we plant potatoes in Europe: in regular, perfectly straight rows, and between each of these there is an interval of free space in which are already sprouting a peculiar species of beans, which will spring up when the field has been reaped. That green surface which might be taken for sprouting corn is a field of millet, which was sown in March and will be ripe in September.

Millet is eaten by the natives in as large quantities as wheat, they grind it into flour, and make cakes or porridge of it.

On an adjacent plain there is a laborers tilling the ground by means of a small plough drawn by one horse. In the fertile soil he will sow the seed of the cottontree, and in September or October each seed will have produced a plant two or three feet high, hulen with twenty capsules arrived at maturity. Several white birds of the stork or heron family seem to be working in concert with the agriculturist, they follow him about gravely, and, by plunging their long beaks into the half-opened furrow, they destroy the larva which the plough has just turned up.

In the depth of the valley are rice paddies, which were laid under water about a month ago by the opening of the sluice gates of the irrigation canals. While in this state, the soil is broken up by the plough, and trodden by the feet of the oxen and the laborers, the latter treading up to their calves in the clay, and breaking the stubborn clumps with pickaxes. When the earth has been mashed into a kind of liquid paste, men and women go step by step along the dykes of the enclosure, and throw in handfuls of seed on the square spaces destined to form the nursery ground. Then these are turned over with a kind of rake, in order to distribute and bury the seed. Now the water has subsided, the nursery ground puts forth its thick, close crop, and the cultivators tear it up, roots and stems together, to transplant them carefully in the large squares of soft earth not yet utilised, in tufts arranged in a checquered pattern at regular intervals. There the rice will grow and ripen, to be cut in the month of October.

Until then it has to dread the pretty little red- and white-breasted birds that fall like hail on the grainladen stems, shake the ripe fruit to the ground, and set to their work of pillage with shrill notes of joy, dancing on their little feet after a fashion full of charm for the impartial observer, but which inspires the proprietor with far different feelings. The persecuted rice growers resort to all kinds of scarecrows, which they set up at the most seriously menaced points, but without much apparent effect on the morals of the thriving birds. In one place, a complete network of cords of plaited straw, garnished with swinging appendages of the same material, is fixed on poles, and extended above the rice field, forming a perfectly efficacious method of prevention, provided that it is kept in incessant motion. This is the task of a boy, who, when there is not sufficient wind to shake the net, pulls the cord attached to it, like a bell rope, and thus keeps it going. The child sits in a lofty seat, perched on four bamboos, under a little roof formed of reeds.

Several kinds of rice are grown in Japan. That of the plains is the most highly esteemed, that of the hills does not require to be so long submerged as the former, but I have seen it subjected, in the spring, to processes of irrigation which have cost much labour, in the formation of reservoirs on the upper level of the hill, and the establishment of numerous canals, discharging themselves on all the terraces prepared for rice culture. Each terrace thus converted into a rice ground will bear, next autumn, wheat or millet. The Japanese may perhaps clear some mountain land now and then, but they will never leave land capable of being tilled, fallow.

The tea-plant is not cultivated in our district. It is occasionally met with under certain favorable circumstances, but the real tea districts are several days' journey north and west of the bay. We are much nearer to the silk-growing districts, and there would he nothing to prevent the development of this industry in our immediate vicinity, if there were sufficient space for the cultivation of the mulberry tree. It strikes me, in short, that the population by whom I am surrounded, and the inhabitants of the southern coasts of Japan generally, leave to the natives of the interior the production of the most valuable articles of commerce, such as silk, tea, and even cotton, which is not very abundant on our coasts, while they devote themselves, some to fishing and water-carriage, and others to agriculture in its strict sense—the production of cereals and leguminous and oleaginous plants, also to horticulture, and the growth of flax, straw, reeds, and bamboos.

Among the peasant population of the fertile valleys that border Edo Bay, one frequently meets men of a more vigorous race, whose aspect, though kindly, seems to denote a certain independence of character or manner of life. These are the "mountain people," or the inhabitants of the Hakone mountains, at the foot of Fuji-*yama*. The business that brings them down to the plains is very various in its nature. For some, it is dealing in wood for ships and building, for others, it is dealing in firewood. Some are carrying baggage on packhorses from the provinces in the interior to such or such a port in the bay, others are employed in hauling the canal boats, and among them recruits are made for a select tribe of hunters, as well as for a portion of the *shōgun*'s troops of the line, i.e. the infantry companies, among whom European arms of precision have been introduced.

Unfortunately, the country inhabited by these passing guests is almost entirely inaccessible to strangers. If certain native statements are to be believed, bridges, aqueducts, and dams of most marvellous construction exist there, which baffle the imagination when one thinks of the imperfection of the instruments by which they have been made. The resources which the Japanese possess in raw material are not accorded to our climates. The bamboo, for instance, furnishes a natural conduit for hydraulic purposes, whose excellence yields to no product of modern industry. It is employed in the formation of suspension bridges in the place of ware. In the mountains of Kyushu there is a bridge, flung from one rock to another across a deep abyss, by means of a hanging staircase formed of huge pieces of bamboo laid in line, and fitted over one another longitudinally. The Japanese traverse great rivers on bridges made of casks, and managed by straw ropes. They cross terrific ravines by bridges of rope, and even by means of a single rope, along which slips a kind of aerial ferry boat.

In a country like theirs, where the government maintains only one public highway—the great military road called the Tōkaidō[1]—the inhabitants, reduced to their own resources, strive to establish the communications

1 In fact, the Bakufu oversaw the maintenance of all the five major highroads—the Tōkaidō, Nakasendō, Nikkōkaidō, Okushūkaidō, and the Kōshūkaidō—throughout the Edo period. Initially supervision of their maintenance, which was largely allocated to villages and towns along the route, was the task of the chief financial officer(s) (*kanjō bugyō*), but in 1659 this became the sole task of the *dōchū bugyō*.

21

they require at the least possible cost. Hence the infinite variety of their contrivances for transport by land and by water. A curious specimen of the latter is the means devised to enable the women who are engaged in rice cultivation to cross the submerged lands. Four tubs, fastened together between the angles of two crossed planks, are packed with as many persons and as large a quantity of provisions as this singular equipage can accommodate, and two of the passengers propel it with poles. The same talent for utilizing the simplest means of action, the most primitive instruments, the most elementary processes, is equally to be traced in the arts and handicrafts of Japan. But there is a very important part of their social life either escapes us or which it is very difficult for us to study. We can only see the people at work in the fields and in some of the village sheds. The docks, the workshops, and the factories in the industrial cities, the artistic conceptions, and the most original productions of their autonomic civilization, are carefully hidden from us by the police restrictions of a jealous government. Nevertheless, little by little the light is coming, and a day will soon dawn when, in this respect too Japan shall be opened to the investigations of Science.

The People

The countryside may be reached from Benten-*dōri* without passing through the city. Beyond the precincts of the holy place, a wide pathway supported on piles forms a road alongside the river. From this road, which leads to a suburb occupied by poor artisans, and terminated by a military guard house and a customs station, we look down on the low streets and the marsh of Yokohama. A handsome wooden bridge, built on piles sufficiently high to permit the passage of sailing boats, crosses the river, and joins the footpath on the left bank.

By following this footpath to the north-east, we reach the high road of Kanagawa. And by taking the south-east direction, we come to the country roads leading to the Bay of the Mississippi.

The country is covered on every side with cultivated land, and the habitations are exceedingly numerous. The isolated houses near the road, and those which border on the village streets, are generally open, and may, so to speak, be seen through. The inhabitants, in order to establish currents of air, slide the screens that form their walls into the grooves on the right and left, so that the interiors of their houses are freely exhibited to the sight of the passers-by.

Under such conditions it is not difficult to form a correct idea of household life, and to observe the distinctive characters of the national type, as well as the domestic manners of the native population.

The conventional separation between classes in Japanese society does not rest on essential difference of race, or of modes of life.

From the height of the hill on which the residence of the governors of

Kanagawa is situated I have more than once had occasion to examine and observe, on one side, some buildings set apart for the dwellings of the *yakunin*, and on the other groups of houses or cottages belonging to artisans and cultivators. In the courtyards, formed by divisions made of planks which separate the military caste from the others, I remarked exactly the same habits, the same modes of life, which I saw publicly in action in the courtyards of the plebeians. My later observation of the houses of the high government functionaries only confirms me in the belief that we may reduce the chief types and the domestic manners of the whole population of the centre of the empire—that is to say, of the three great islands of Kyushu, Shikoku, and Honshu—to certain general features.

There is more difference in height between the men and the women of Japan than in those of Europe. According to the observations of Dr. Otto Gottlieb Mohnike, formerly physician to the Dutch Factory of Deshima, the average height of the men is five feet one inch, or five feet two inches (French measurement), and that of the women from four feet one inch to four feet three inches.

The Japanese, without being precisely disproportioned, have generally large heads, rather sunk in the shoulders, wide chests, long bodies, narrow hips, short and thin legs, small feet, and slight and remarkably beautiful hands. Their retreating foreheads and large and prominent cheekbones make their faces represent the geometrical figure of the trapeze rather than that of the oval. The cavities of the eyes being very shallow, and the cartilage of the nose rather flattened, the eyes in almost every case are more on the surface than those of the European, and sometimes very narrow. But, nevertheless, the general effect is not that of the Chinese or Mongol type. The head of the Japanese is large, the face is long, and on the average more regular. Finally, the nose is more prominent, better formed, and sometimes even aquiline. According to Mohnike, the Japanese head is that of the Turanian race.

All the Japanese population, without exception, have fine, thick, straight, and lustrous black hair. The women's hair is shorter than in the European and Malay countries. The Japanese have thick beards, but they shave at least every second day. The color of their skin varies according to the different classes of society, from the copper tints of the interior of Java to the sunburnt white of the natives of southern Europe. The predominant shade is olive-brown, but it never resembles the yellow tint of the Chinese. Unlike those of Europeans, the face and hands of the Japanese are generally less colored than the body, little children and young persons of both sexes have rosy complexions, red cheeks, and the same indications of robust health we like to see in persons of our own race.

The women have fairer complexions than the men, we saw several persons of rank, and even in the middle classes, who were perfectly white, the ladies of the aristocracy regard excessive paleness as a mark of distinction.

Both men and women have black eyes, white and perfect teeth, separated by regular interstices, and slightly projecting. It is the custom for married women to blacken their teeth. In this we trace a tradition of Java, where the women file their teeth down to the gums, or of the Malay country in general, where everyone has black teeth, produced by the use of the betel.

The national garment of the Japanese is the "*kimono.*" It is a kind of open dressing gown, made a little longer and more ample for women than for men. It is crossed at the waist by means of a sash, which for men is made of a straight and narrow piece of silk—for women, of a large piece of material elegantly tied at the back.

The Japanese wear no linen, but they bathe every day. The women wear a chemise of red silk crape. In summer, the peasants, the fishermen, the artisans, and the coolies do their work in a state of almost complete nudity, and the women merely wear a single petticoat. During the rains they wear large cloaks of straw or oilpaper, and hats of bamboo bark, made like those of Java, in the form of shields.

In winter the workingmen wear a jacket and trousers of blue cotton under the *kimono*, and the women one or several wadded mantles, but generally there is no difference between their costumes, excepting in the nature of the materials. The nobles alone have a right to wear silk, and only dress richly to go to court, or to make visits of ceremony. The officers of the government, and the *yakunin* on duty, wear wide trailing trousers. And the *kimono* by an overcoat with large sleeves, which only comes down to the hips, and is rather elegantly cut. Everyone wears the same coverings for the feet, which consist of sandals of plaited straw (*zōri*), or wooden (*geta*) slippers fastened by a cord in which the great toe is caught. When the roads are muddy, the people wear a simple wooden sole, resting on two smaller pieces placed crosswise. During the greater portion of the year the working people merely use straw sandals. Each, on returning to his own house, or on presenting himself at that of a stranger, removes his socks or his sandals and leaves them at the door.

The floors of the Japanese houses are constantly covered with mats. As they are all of the same size, which is so invariable that the mat is used as a standard measure—it is never difficult to arrange them in an apartment. They are uniformly six feet three inches long, three feet two inches wide, and four inches thick. They are made of rice straw, very carefully plaited, by combining them with the grooves made in the floor and with the sliding screens which form the walls of the rooms, the Japanese divide their habitation into small or large rooms. But the dimensions are always regular, and they modify this distribution exactly as it pleases them, without trouble, and never departing from the exactly symmetrical lines.

The mat dispenses with all other furniture, it is the mattress on which the Japanese passes the night, wrapped up in an ample dressing gown, and under a large wadded counterpane, with his head resting on a little bolster made of strips of bamboo, on it he sets out the utensils of lacquer and porcelain used at his meals, on it the bare feet of his children tread, it is the divan where, crouching on his heels, surrounded by his friends and his guests, all crouching like him, he indulges in interminable talk, drinking a decoction of tea unmingled with any other ingredient, and smoking tobacco out of microscopic pipes.

In all the inns of Japan we find a moveable floor like a great table, covered with mats and raised only a foot above the ground. On this the traveller sits or crouches, eats, drinks, takes a siesta, and chats with his neighbors. The Japanese house is nothing more than this table brought to perfection, a *reposoir*, a temporary refuge in which to take shelter when the labours of the street and the country are terminated. But it is not the centre of existence, if we may be permitted to use that expression at all in speaking of a people who live from day to day, forgetful of yesterday, not caring for tomorrow.

One day, when 1 had been listening to the recitation of half a dozen of the young boys in our neighborhood, who were squatting in front of their schoolmaster, I asked what was the name of the exercise they were repeating in chorus. I was told they were practising to recite the *iroha*, a sort of alphabet in which not the vowels and consonants, but the fundamental signs of the Japanese language, are collected and grouped in four lines. The number of those sounds is fixed at forty-eight, and instead of classifying them in grammatical elements according to the organs of speech, they have been made into a little piece of poetry, whose first word, *iroha*, gives its name to the alphabet. As nearly as I can reproduce the sense of the rhyme, this is it:

> *Color and odor alike pass away.*
> *In our world nothing is permanent.*
> *The present day has disappeared*
> *in the profound abyss of nothingness.*
> *It is but the pale image of a dream:*
> *it causes us not the least regret.*

This national alphabet told me more of the character of the Japanese people than I might have found in volumes. For centuries the generations who were departing repeated to the generation who were coming, "There is nothing permanent in this world, the present passes like a dream, and its flight causes not the slightest trouble." That this popular philosophy of noth-ingness does not give full satisfaction to the needs of the soul, is quite evident when we consider how largely the manifestations of religious sentiment have developed of late, nevertheless, it is probable that it acts incessantly as a latent force, and its influence is felt in all the details of life.

The children profit most by the way of life to which this gives rise. In the first place, it is granted by everyone that the child ought to have its own way. Fathers and mothers derive their pleasure from the observance of this natural law. Every means of enjoyment for children, every subject of their amusement, becomes a source of personal satisfaction to the parents, they give themselves up to it with all their hearts, and it suits the children admirably. Travellers who have said that Japanese children never cry, have stated with very little exaggeration of expression a perfectly real phenomenon. It is explained by circumstances to which I have alluded, as well as by certain external conditions.

The Japanese is husband to only one wife, who passes almost without transition from her doll to her child, and preserves for a long time her natural infantile character. On the other hand, the national custom does not permit her to bring up her baby too carefully. She is obliged to expose it to the atmospheric influences, carrying it into the air every day, even at noon, with its head shaven, and perfectly naked. In order to carry the child about as long as possible without much fatigue, the woman places it on her back, fastening it like a package between her chemise and the collar of her kimono. Thus the wives of the peasants may constantly be seen working in the fields with a little head wagging about between their shoulders. In the house the children may be left to themselves without any uneasiness, they can roll about among the mats, crawling on all fours and trying to stand upright, because there is no furniture against which they can hurt themselves, nor any object which they can knock down or break.

Their companions are the domestic animals—little pug-dogs with short legs and tremendously fat bodies, and a particular species of cat with white fur marked with yellow and black stripes, who are exceedingly bad mousers, very idle, and very affectionate. Like the cats of Java and the Isle of Man, these animals have no tails.

Every family in easy circumstances possesses an aquarium, containing fish—red, silver, gold, transparent—some round as a ball, others ornamented with a long wide tail or fin, which performs the office of a rudder, and which floats about like a piece of extremely fine gauze. In all the houses there are cages made of bamboo bark, constructed on the models of the most elegant habitations, and containing large butterflies shut up there on a bed of flowers, or grasshoppers, in whose strident and monotonous cry the natives take great delight.

Such are the surroundings amid which the Japanese child grows up without any restraint in the paternal house, which is merely a sort of shady playground.

His parents are prodigal of toys, and games, and entertainments, as much for their own enjoyment as in the interest of his education. His lessons, properly speaking, consist in singing in chorus, at the top of his voice, the iroha, and drawing with his brush and Chinese ink the first letters of the alphabet, then words, then phrases. There is no compulsion and no precipitation about these lessons, because they are certain things of undeniable utility that can only be acquired by long practice. No one ever thinks of depriving his child of the benefits of instruction. There are no scholastic rules, no measures of coercion for recalcitrant parents, and nevertheless the whole adult population can read, write, and calculate. There is something estimable in the pedagogic regime of Japan.

Kamakura

The environs of Kamakura are those of a great city. But the great city itself exists no longer. Rich vegetation covers the inequalities of the soil that has evidently accumulated over ruins, overthrown walls, and canals now filled up. Antique avenues of trees stretch beyond waste groves overgrown with brambles. These avenues formerly led to palaces, of which there is now no trace. In Japan, even palaces, being for the most part built of wood, leave no ruins after their fall.

At Kamakura the *shōgun* had established their residence. Under the name of *shōgun* we recall the generals-in-chief, temporal lieutenants of the theocratic emperor. They governed Japan, under the supremacy of the emperor, from the end of the twelfth century to the commencement of the seventeenth, from Minamoto Yoritomo, who was the founder of their power, to Tokugawa Ieyasu, the thirty-second *shōgun*, who made Edo the political capital of Japan, and created a present dynasty, whose last representative adopted the title of *shōgun* in 1854.

At the present time we find at Kamakura the pantheon of the glories of Japan. It is composed of a majestic collection of sacred buildings that have always been spared by the fury of civil war. They are placed under the invocation of Hachiman, one of the great national *kami*. Hachiman belongs to the heroic period of the empire of the emperors. His mother was the Empress Jingū, who effected the conquest of the three kingdoms of Korea, and to whom divine honorus are rendered. Each year, on the ninth day of the ninth month, a solemn procession to the tomb consecrated to her at Fujimi, in the country of Yamashiro, commemorates her glorious deeds.

Jingū herself surnamed her son Hatsuran, "Eight Banners," in consequence of a sign that appeared in the heavens at the birth of the child. Thanks to the education she gave him, she made him the bravest of her soldiers and the most skilful of her generals. When she had attained the age of one hundred years she transmitted the sceptre and crown of the emperors to her son, in the year 270 of our era. He was then seventy-one years old. Under the name of Ōjin he reigned gloriously for forty-three years, and was raised, after his death, to the rank of a protecting genius of the empire. He is especially revered as the patron of soldiers. In the annual festivals dedicated to him, Japan celebrates the memory of the heroes who have died for their country. The popular processions that take place on this occasion revive the ancient pomps of *kami* worship. Even the horses formerly destined for sacrifice are among the cortage. But instead of being immolated, they are turned loose on the race-course.

Most of the great cities of Japan possess a shrine dedicated to Hachiman. That of Kamakura is distinguished above all the others by the trophies it contains. Two vast buildings are required for the display of this national wealth. There, it is said, are preserved the spoils of the Korean and the Mongol invasions, also objects taken from the Portuguese colonies and the Christian communities of Japan at the epoch when the Portuguese were expelled, and the Japanese Christians were exterminated by order of the *shōgun*.

No European has ever yet been permitted to view the trophies of Kamakura. While all European states like to display the treasures they have seized or won in their frontier and dynastic wars, Japan hides all monuments of its military glory from foreigners. They are kept in reserve, like a family treasure, in venerable sanctuaries, to which no profane feet ever find access.

On approaching the shrine of Hachiman we perceived that our arrival had been announced, and that the monks were closing the shutters of their treasure house.

The shrines of Hachiman are approached by long lines of those great cedar trees that form the avenues to all places of worship in Japan. As we advance along the avenue on the Kanazawa side, chapels multiply themselves along the road, and to the left, on the sacred hills, we also come in sight of the oratories and commemorative stones that mark the stations of the processions, on the right the horizon is closed by the mountain, with its grottos, its streams, and its pine groves. After we have crossed the river by a fine wooden bridge, we find ourselves suddenly at the entrance of another alley, which leads from the seaside, and occupies a large street. This is the principal avenue, intersected by three gigantic *torii*, and it opens on the grand square in front of the chief staircase of the main buildings of the shrine. The precinct of the sacred place extends into the street, and is surrounded on three sides by a low wall of solid masonry, surmounted by a barrier of wood painted red and black. Two steps lead to the first level.

There is nothing to be seen there but the houses of the monks, arranged like the side-scenes of a theater, amid trees planted along the barrier wall, with two great oval ponds occupying the centre of the square. They are connected with each other by a large canal crossed by two parallel bridges, each equally remarkable in its way. That on the right is of white granite, and it describes an almost perfect semicircle, so that when one sees it for the first time one supposes it is intended for some sort of geometrical exercise. But I suppose it is in reality a bridge of honor, reserved for the gods and the good genii who come to visit the shrine. The bridge on the left is quite flat, constructed of wood covered with red lacquer, with balusters and other ornaments in old polished copper. The pond crossed by the stone bridge is covered with magnificent white lotus flowers—the pond crossed by the wooden bridge with red lotus flowers. Among the leaves of the flowers we saw numbers of fish, some red and others like mother of pearl, with glittering fins, swimming about in water of crystal clearness. The black tortoise glides among the great water plants and clings to their stems.

After having thoroughly enjoyed this most attractive spectacle, we go on towards the second enclosure. It is raised a few steps higher than the first, and, as it is protected by an additional sanctity, it is only to be approached through the gate of the divine guardians of the sanctuary. This building, which stands opposite the bridges, contains two monstrous idols, placed side by side in the centre of the edifice. They are sculptured in wood, and are covered from head to foot with a thick coating of vermilion. Their grinning faces and their enormous busts are spotted all over with innumerable pieces of chewed paper, which the native visitors throw at them when passing, without any more formality than would be used by a number of schoolboys out for a holiday. Nevertheless, it is considered a very serious act on the part of the pilgrims. It is the means by which they make the prayer written on the sheet of chewed paper reach its address, and when they wish to recommend anything to the gods very strongly indeed, they bring as an offering a pair of straw slippers plaited with regard to the size of the feet of the colossus, and hang them on the iron railings within which the statues are enclosed. Articles of this kind, suspended by thousands to the bars, remain there until they fall away in time, and it may be supposed that this curious ornamentation is anything but beautiful.

Here a lay brother of the monks approached us, and his interested views were easily enough detected by his bearing. We hastened to assure him that we required nothing from his good offices, except access to an enclosed building. With a shake of his head, so as to make us understand that we were asking for an impossibility, he simply set himself to follow us about with the mechanical precision of a subaltern. He was quite superfluous, but we did not allow his presence to interfere with our admiration.

A high terrace, reached by a long stone staircase, surmounted the second enclosure. It is sustained by a Cyclopean wall, and in its turn supports the principal shrine as well as the habitations of the priests. The grey roofs of all these different buildings stand out against the sombre forest of cedars and pines. On our left are the buildings of the treasury, one of them has a pyramidal roof surmounted by a turret of bronze most elegantly worked. At the foot of the great terrace is the chapel of the ablutions. On our right stands a tall pagoda, constructed on the principle of the Chinese pagodas, but in a more sober and severe style. The first stage, of a quadrangular form, is supported by pillars, the second stage consists of a vast circular gallery which, though extremely massive, seems to rest simply on a pivot. A painted roof, terminated by a tall spire of cast bronze, embellished with pendants of the same metal, completes the effect of this strange but exquisitely pro-portioned building.

All the doors of the buildings I have enumerated are in good taste. The fine proportions, the rich brown coloring of the wood, which is almost the only material employed in their construction, is enhanced by a few touches of red and dragon green, and the effect of the whole is perfect—add to the picture a frame of ancient trees and the extreme brilliancy of the sky, for the atmosphere of Japan is the most transparent in the world.

We went beyond the pagoda to visit a bell tower, where we were shown a large bell beautifully engraved, and an oratory on each side containing three golden images, a large one in the centre, and two small ones at either side. Each was surrounded by a nimbus. This beautiful shrine, the Tsurugaoka Hachiman-gū, is consecrated to the *kami* Hachiman. But it is quite evident that the religious customs of India have supplanted the ancient worship— we had several proofs of this fact. When we were about to turn back we were solicited by the lay brother to go with him a little further. We complied, and he stopped us under a tree laden with ex-votos, at the foot of which stands a block of stone, surrounded by a barrier. This stone, which is probably indebted to the chisels of the monks for its peculiar form, is venerated by the multitude, and largely endowed with ex-voto offerings. Like the peoples of the extreme East the Japanese are very superstitious, a fact of which we had abundant evidence on this and other occasions.

The Hase Kannon temple towards which we directed our steps on leaving the avenue of the Tsurugaoka Hachiman-gū, immediately diverted our thoughts from the grandeur of this picture. It is admirably situated on the summit of a promontory, whence we overlook the whole Bay of Kamakura. But it is always sad to come, in the midst of beautiful nature, on a so-called holy place which inspires nothing but disgust.

The principal sanctuary, at first sight, did not strike us as remarkable. Insignificant golden idols stand on the high altar. And in a side chapel there is an image of the god of wealth, armed with a miner's hammer. But when the monks who received us conducted us behind the high altar, and from there into a sort of cage as dark as a prison and as high as a tower, they lighted two lanterns, and stuck them at the end of a long pole. Then, by this glimmering light, which entirely failed to disperse the shades of the roof, we perceived that we were standing in front of an enormous idol of gilt wood, about twelve yards high, holding in its right hand a sceptre, in its left a lotus, and wearing a tiara composed of three rows of heads, representing the inferior divinities. This gigantic idol belongs to the religion of the auxiliary gods of the Buddhist mythology, the Amida and the Kannon, intercessors who collect the prayers of men and transmit them to heaven.

By means of similar religious conceptions, the monks strike a superstitious terror into the imaginations of their followers, and succeed in keeping them in a state of perpetual fear and folly.

We then went to see the Daibutsu, which is the wonder of Kamakura. This building is dedicated to the Daibutsu, that is to say, to the great Buddha, and may be regarded as the most finished work of Japanese genius, from the double points of view of art and religious sentiment. The Tsurugaoka Hachiman-gū had already given us a remarkable example of the use which native art makes of nature in producing that impression of religious majesty which in our northern climates is effected by Gothic architecture. The temple of Daibutsu differs considerably from the first we had seen. Instead of the great dimensions, instead of the illimitable space which seemed to stretch from portal to portal down to the sea, a solitary and mysterious retreat prepares the mind for some supernatural revelation. The road leads far away from every habitation, in the direction of the mountain it winds about between hedges of tall shrubs. Finally, we see nothing before us but the high road, going up and up in the midst of foliage and flowers, then it turns in a totally different direction, and all of a sudden, at the end of the alley, we perceive a gigantic brazen divinity, squatting with joined hands, and the head slightly bent forward, in an attitude of contemplative ecstasy. The involuntary amazement produced by the aspect of this great image soon gives place to admiration. There is an irresistible charm in the attitude of the Daibutsu, as well as in the harmony of its proportions. The noble simplicity of its garments and the calm purity of its features are in perfect accord with the sentiment of serenity inspired by its presence. A grove, consisting of some beautiful groups of trees, forms the enclosure of the sacred place, whose silence and solitude are never disturbed. The small cell of the attendant priest can hardly be discerned amongst the foliage. The altar, on which a little incense is burning at its feet, is composed of a small brass table ornamented by two lotus vases of the same metal, and beautifully wrought. The steps of the altar are composed of large slabs forming regular lines. The blue of the sky, the deep shadow of the statue, the sombre color of the brass, the brilliancy of the flowers, the varied verdure of the hedges and the groves, fill this solemn retreat with the richest effect of light and color.

The idol of the Daibutsu, with the platform which supports it, is twenty yards high, it is far from equal in elevation to the statue of St. Charles Borromeo, which may be seen from Arona on the borders of Lake Maggidre, but which affects the spectator no more than a trigonometrical signal post. The interiors of these two colossal statues have been utilized. The European tourists seat themselves in the nose of the holy cardinal. The Japanese descend by a secret staircase into the foundations of their Daibutsu, and there they find a peaceful oratory, whose altar is lighted by a ray of sunshine admitted through an opening in the folds of the mantle at the back of the idol's neck. It would be idle to discuss to what extent the Buddha of Kamakura resembles the Buddha of history, but it is important to remark that he is conformable to the Buddha of tradition.

The Buddhists have made one authentic and sacramental image of the founder of their religion, covered with characters carefully numbered, with thirty-two principal signs, and eighty secondary marks, so that it may be transmitted to future ages in all its integrity. The Japanese idol conforms in all essential respects to this established type of the great Hindu reformer. It scrupulously reproduces the pose, the meditative attitudes, thus it was that the sage joined his hands, the fingers straightened, and thumb resting against thumb, thus he squatted, the legs bent and gathered up one over the other, the right foot lying on the left knee. The broad, smooth brow is also to be recognized, and the hair forming a multitude of short curls. Even the singular protuberance of the skull, which slightly disfigures the top of the head, exists in the statue, and also a tuft of white hairs between the eyebrows, indicated by a little rounded excrescence in the metal.

All these marks, however, do not constitute the physiognomy, the expression of the personage. In this respect the Daibutsu of Kamakura has nothing in common with the fantastic dolls worshipped in China under the name of Buddhas, and the fact appears worthy of notice, because Buddhism was introduced into Japan from China.

The first effect of Buddhist preaching in Japan must have been to arouse curiosity among the islanders, who are as inquisitive and restless as the Hindoos are taciturn and contemplative.

What a vast field of exploration for minds that were only making their first voyage of discovery in the regions of metaphysics! As they did not feel any impatience to plunge into Nirvana, they were chiefly interested in finding out what was to come to pass between death and final extinction. With the assistance of the monks, a certain number of accepted ideas about the soul, death, and the life to come, were put in circulation in the towns and in the villages, without prejudice, it must be understood, to all that had been taught by ancestral wisdom concerning the ancient gods and the venerable national *kami*.

The soul of man, it was said, is like a floating vapor, indissoluble, having the form of a tiny worm, and a thin thread of blood that runs from the top of the head to the extremity of the tail. If it were closely observed it might be seen to escape from the house of death, at the moment when the dying person heaves his last sigh. At all times, the cracking of the panel may be heard as the soul passes through it. Where does it go? No one knows. But it cannot fail to be received by the ministering servants of the great judge of hell. They bring it before his tribunal, and the judge causes it to kneel before a mirror, in which it beholds all the evil of which it has been guilty. This is a phenomenon occasionally produced on earth: a comedian in Edo, who had committed a murder, could not look into his mirror without his gaze being met by the livid face of his victim.

Souls, laden with crime, wander in one or other of the eighteen concentric circles of hell, according to the gravity of their offenses. Souls in process of purification sojourn in a purgatory whose lid they may lift up when they can do so without fear of falling, and resume the progressive course of their pilgrimage. In the case of a woman who, being deserted, drowned herself with her child, she is popularly believed to present herself before all wayfarers by the side of the marsh, holding up the infant, in protest against her betrayers as the real author of her crime. Finally, there are souls who return to the places they have inhabited, or to the resting-place of their mortal remains.

Ghost stories, terrible tales, books illustrated with pictures representing hell or apparitions of demons, have multiplied in Japan with such profusion, that the popular imagination is completely possessed by them. The patron of literature of this kind, according to the national mythology, is Tengu, the god of dreams, a burlesque winged genius, whose headdress is an extinguisher with a golden handle. He leads the nocturnal revelry of all the objects, sacred or profane, which can fill the imagination of man. The refuge of death itself is not closed against him. The candelabra bend their heads, pierced with luminous holes, with a measured motion. The stone tortoises that bear the epitaphs move in a grim, orderly march, and grinning skeletons, clad in their shrouds, join the fantastic measure, waving about them the holy water brush that drives away evil spirits.

In spite of some difference in style, and of its exceptional dimensions, the noble Japanese statue is the fellow of those of which great numbers are to be seen in the islands of Java and Ceylon, those sacred refuges which were opened to Buddhism when it was expelled from India. There the type of the hero of contemplation is preserved most religiously, and appears under its most exquisite form, in marvellous images of basalt, granite, and clay, generally above the human stature, This type, for the most part conventional, although perfectly authentic in the eyes of faith, is, especially for the Sri Lankan priests, who are devoted to the art of statuary, the unique subject of the indefatigable labour by which they strive to realize ideal perfection. They have in fact produced work of such purity as has hardly been surpassed by the Madonnas of Raphael.

The Tōkaidō

To Tokugawa Ieyasu is due the merit of having made Edo the political capital of Japan, and the obligatory residence of the noble families of the empire. At that epoch, at the commencement of the seventeenth century, Edo was not equal in importance to the pontifical Kyoto, nor to Osaka, the centre of commerce, nor even to Nagasaki. But, like the last city, it has the advantage of a strategical position, easily defended on the land side, and regarded as impregnable on that of the sea. The German scientist Engelbert Kaempfer, who on two occasions went with an embassy of the Dutch India Company to Kyoto and to Edo, reckons that in the line of the Tōkaidō, or close to it, there are thirty-three great cities with fortresses and fifty-seven small towns unfortified, without mentioning an infinite number of villages and hamlets. It takes no less than from twenty-five to thirty days to go from Nagasaki to Edo, by the Tōkaidō, using the means of transport customary among the natives, who know no other than the horse or the palanquin.

There are two sorts of palanquin or *kago*. One requires four bearers for long journeys, is a large, heavy box, in which one may sit with tolerable comfort. The sides are in lacquered wood, and contain two sliding doors. Although this palanquin is, par excellence, the vehicle of the nobility, it has no ornaments, and is used by the ladies of the middle class and by the registered courtesans, because both occupy a certain position of fortune and consideration in society. The other is a light litter of bamboo, open on both sides, it requires only two bearers, who always walk with a rapid and regular step. They rest for one minute out of twenty. When they go back, each carries in his turn the palanquin, suspended at the end of a pole, over his shoulder.

The packhorses intended for the transport of merchandise and of travellers go slowly behind their drivers, the head bent, and attached by a strap that passes under the body to the cord that goes round the animal. The Japanese, instead of shoeing their horses, wrap their hoofs in a little mat, which only lasts one day. According as these mats wear out, they are thrown aside, and immediately replaced, and large provisions of them always make part of the baggage. Foot passengers do the same with their sandals of plaited straw, so that all the roads of Japan are covered with these relics.

The Tōkaidō is crossed in several places by arms of the sea and by rapid rivers. Large boats do duty as coaches, and cross the strait that separates the island of Kyushu from Shimonoseki in two hours. Most of the travellers, and even pilgrims, profit by the great merchant junks of the Inland Sea to make the journey from Shimonoseki to Kobe. It is only half a day's journey from Kobe to Osaka, and one day from Osaka by river to Kyoto. Between this city and Edo lie the most picturesque portions of the road.

Travellers cross the rivers in flat boats, or on the shoulders of porters. These porters form a corporation, which indemnifies the traveller in case of personal accident or loss of baggage. With the exception of a girdle tattooing suffices for their clothing, according to custom among the coolies of Japan. The subjects of this process are heroic, such as the strife of Yamato with the dragon, the tribunal of hell, and the image of that incomparable soldier who, when his head was falling under the sword, tore off his enemies' armour with his teeth.

The fare is always extremely moderate, and varies according to whether eight men are employed to carry the palanquin, or four men with a litter, two men with a stretcher, or a simple porter. In the latter case, which is the most frequent, the traveller seats himself astride the bearer's neck, and the latter takes him by both legs, and, telling him to sit steadily, steps into the water warily and firmly. Sometimes a sudden rise of the river intercepts the passage, and then the travellers install themselves in the teahouses on the shore, from where they watch the water until the porters come to tell them the ford is practicable.

Three days' journey from Edo, the Tōkaidō passes by the foot of Mount Fuji, from which it is only separated by the lake of Hakone. Thousands of pilgrims go annually in procession to the summit of the marvellous mountain, where they are received by the monks of a convent built at the very edge of the crater, which opened for the first time 286 years before the birth of Christ and vomited its last lava in 1707.

The hills of Hakone, covered with forests in which large game abound, give access to no other road than that of the Tōkaidō. All the roads of the provinces to the west and south of Edo are connected with this great artery, while this one ends in a narrow defile, provided with heavy barriers and fortified guard houses. Here all travellers have to exhibit their passports, and submit their effects to the inspection of the government officers. Neither the *daimyō*, nor their imposing suites, can exempt them from these formalities, whose special object is the prevention of the clandestine conveyance of arms into the provinces, no less than attempts at evasion on the part of the noble ladies whose birth and the laws of *shōgun* condemn them to reside at Edo.

Not content with these precautions, which do not extend to the northern provinces, Ieyasu and his successors thought it necessary to protect the approaches to their capital on that side by a long wall, at whose gates an inspection is made by the custom house and police officers.

Beyond the hills of Hakone, the Tōkaidō overlooks Sagami Bay, towards Edo Bay, which it joins at the village of Kanagawa, opposite Yokohama. All these localities have been the scenes of assassinations, committed on inoffensive foreigners of different nations by men belonging to the class of the *samurai*, or Japanese nobles having the privilege of carrying two swords.

Major George Waler Baldwin and Lieutenant Robert Bird, English officers, were murdered not far from the statue of the Daibtsu of Kamakura. The corpse of Lieutenant Camus, a French officer, was found horribly mutilated along the Tōkaidō, at the entrance of the village of Hodogaya. An English merchant, Charles Lennox Richardson, was also killed along the Tōkaidō, at the hamlet of Namamugi. Two Russian officers, and, shortly after, two captains of the Dutch merchant marine, Wessel de Vos and Jasper Nanning Decker, were cut to pieces in the high street of the Japanese city of Yokohama. A Japanese interpreter to the English minister, and the Dutch interpreter of the American legation, Henry Heusken, perished in the streets of Edo. The whole of the British legation had a narrow escape of falling victims to a night attack, which was repelled with great bloodshed. Two English soldiers were killed at their posts in a second attack on the same legation. It is difficult to forget these things when one is residing in the country where they have happened, and above all when cue has installed one's self at Edo.

The government of the *shōgun* is always disposed to dwell on the danger presented by a sojourn in the capital. That does not prevent their adding that the *shōgun* is profoundly humiliated that such a state of things should exist in his country. On the other hand, where he finds himself at a loss for expedients to escape the reception of an embassy, or when he has used eloquence in persuading them to retire, he is particularly anxious to prove to his foreign guests that the fears he has thought it his duty to express are well founded.

Thus, when one goes to Edo by land, one is obliged to accept the escort of a troop of mounted *yakunin*. Ours joined us at the limit assigned to the residents of Yokohama for their exercise towards the north of the bay. We crossed the arm of the sea that separates Benten from Kanagawa in our junk. Our horses were awaiting us in the latter village, and we enjoyed our last hour of liberty by following the Tōkaidō, with its two interminable files of travellers on foot, on horseback, and in palanquins. Those who were going to the capital kept the road to the right, those who were coming back keeping the left.

We halted at the Mandia teahouse, which was crowded with picturesque groups of guests. All along the front are stoves, smoking kettles, tables laden with provisions, active waitresses coming and going on the right and left, distributing lacquered trays with cups of tea, bowls of *sake*, fried fish, cakes, and fruits of the season. Before the threshold, seated on benches, were artizans and coolies fanning themselves, while their wives lit their pipes at the common *hibachi*. Suddenly a movement of horror manifested itself among the guests and the waitresses, a detachment of police officers, escorting a criminal, came to take refreshment. With great haste, boiling tea and *sake* are offered to the two-sworded men, while the coolies, who carried the prisoner in a bamboo basket, without any opening, deposit their burden on the ground, and rub themselves dry with a long piece of crape. As for the unhappy criminal, who could be seen doubled up in his bamboo prison, a man with haggard eyes, dishevelled hair, and bushy beard, he was going to be tortured in the prisons of Edo as a punishment for the evil deeds set forth on a placard that hung from his ignominious basket.

The beautiful little town of Kawasaki boasts of several temples, among which that of the Heiken-*ji* seems to be one of the purest monuments of Buddhist architecture in Japan. I had heard different versions of the worship to which it is consecrated, among others, the miraculous legend reputed of the saint who was the special object of veneration of the faithful in that place. To so high a degree did he possess the virtue of contemplation, that he did not perceive that a coal fire placed near him in a brazier was consuming his hands, while he was absorbed in meditation.

Although the Tōkaidō is in general as fine a road as any of our great European highways, and has the advantage of being bordered over its whole extent by footpaths shaded with fine plantations of trees, it is in the environs of the capital, strange to say, that it is worst kept. One day of rain turns the streets of the numerous villages beyond Kanagawa into gullies. On this point, as on many others, the Japanese display, at the same time, a remarkable intelligence in all their works of civilization, and, when they come to the application of them, a carelessness in detail no less extraordinary.

At length we reach the populous suburbs of Edo. A short halt on the threshold of one of the numerous teahouses of the village of Omori introduces us to a merry company of citizens, accompanied by their wives and children. Other groups, who were making no less noise, were besieging a great toy shop, an infinite variety of playthings for children, fancy straw hats, animals of plaited straw, painted and varnished, were placed in the front. I readily recognized the bear of Hokkaido, the monkey of Japan, the domestic buffalo, the tortoise a hundred years old, dragging like a long tail great tufts of seaweed growing from his shell.

But time pressed, and, the sight of the offing covered with white sails exciting our impatience, we made our way to the sea-board. The road rests on strong stone foundations, but the waves that formerly came up to it are now lost among the reeds and sea plants. On our left is stretched a pine wood, and some cypress groves, over which we noticed great flocks of crows were hovering. Our guides informed us that this is the place of capital executions, Suzugamori—or at least that of the southern quarter of the great city, for there is a second in the northern quarter.

The aspect of the place is exceedingly gloomy. If one is sufficiently fortunate as to escape the sight of mutilated heads or bodies abandoned to the dogs and the birds, one cannot behold, without horror, the great extent of earth covering the last remains of criminals, a granite pillar, bearing I know not what funeral inscription, a platform appropriated to the use of the officers who have to preside at executions, and a gigantic statue of Buddha, a gloomy symbol of implacable expiation and death without consolation.

Immediately after passing the place where the justice of the *shōgun* exhibits his exemplary vengeance to the people, we enter the most ill-famed suburb of Edo, Shinagawa, which commences at two miles south of the city, and joins it at the gates of the Takanawa quarter.

The government has taken measures to provide foreigners coming to Edo, or residing in that city, with a strong escort in passing through Shinagawa, which they are only allowed to do by daylight. The regular population of this neighborhood is inoffensive, being composed for the most part of boatmen, fishermen, and laborers. But they inhabit the cabins that throng the beach, while the two sides of the Tōkaidō are lined almost uninterruptedly with teahouses of the worst kind, which harbour the same scum of society as in the great cities in Europe and America, and in addition a very dangerous class of men proper to the capital of Japan. These are the *rōnin*, officers without employment, belonging to the caste of the *samurai*, and consequently preserving the right of wearing two swords. Some of them are men of good family, who have been turned out of their homes in consequence of the debauchery of their lives. Others have lost, through misconduct, their place in the service of the *shōgun*, or in the military house of some *daimyō*. Others have been dismissed by a chief, whom evil times has forced to restrict his expenses by the reduction of his personal following.

The *rōnin*, deprived of the pay on which he lived, and knowing no other profession than that of arms, has generally no other resource, while waiting for a new engagement, than to take refuge in these dens of vice, where he repays the hospitality he receives by the vilest kind of industry. The customers whom he attracts add new elements of wickedness to those with which the suburb abounds. A kind of organization of discipline even in disorder is established. There are captains of *rōnin* who hold the bands of wretches in blind subjection, and to whom the mysterious agents, who are the instruments of family vengeance or political hatred among the Japanese nobility, address themselves to get their bloody work done.

Shinagawa is abandoned by the police during the greater part of the night. The women come down on the Tōkaidō, accost belated travellers, and drag them into the inns where they serve. The *rōnin* are so conscious of the state of abjectness in which they live, that, when they come out of their dens, they generally hide their faces under broad-brimmed hats, or wear a piece of crape wrapped round the head, so that the eyes only are visible. It is in this unpleasing neighborhood on the height of the Takanawa quarter that the Japanese government has placed the foreign legations.

Edo

Above all other great cities in the world, Edo seems to be favored by nature in situation, climate, vegetable wealth, and abundance of running water. It is placed at the mouth of two rivers, of which one bathes the Honjo on the east, and the other, passing from north to south through the most populous quarters of the, town, separates the Honjo from the city, and from the two Asakusas.

Two wide streams among seven or eight of less importance flow through the districts that surround the citadel. They are the Arakawa, and the Edo-gawa, basins, tanks, moats. A whole network of irrigating canals, connect these natural watercourses, and cany commercial circulation, popular animation, and the movement and life of the immense capital, into the heart of the city, as well as to the centre and extremities of the Honjo.

Among the number of canals on the sea side of the citadel, that of Nihonbashi holds the first rank, the canal of Kyōbashi holds the second, they are both in the heart of the commercial city.

The most picturesque view of Edo is to be had from its Nihon-*bashi*, the most strongly fortified of the bridges. On turning towards the north, we have on the horizon the white pyramid of Fuji-*yama*, on the right, the city, overlooked by terraces, the parks and the square towers of the residence of the *shōgun*. In the same direction, and as far as its junction with the moats of the citadel, the canal of Nihonbashi is bordered on both banks by innumerable warehouses containing silk, cotton, rice, and *sake*. On our left, beyond the fish market, lie canals, and streets which go down to the Sumida-*gawa*. Hundreds of long boats, laden with wood, coal, bamboo canes, mats, covered baskets, boxes, barrels, and enormous fish, are crossing and recrossing through all the channels of navigation, while the streets seem to be exclusively given up to the people. Occasionally, a string of horses or black oxen heavily laden may be distinguished among the crowd of foot passengers, and sometimes we see heavy waggons carrying four or five layers of skilfully packed bales. These two-wheeled vehicles are drawn by coolies. No other kind of carriage is to be seen. The sound of wooden shoes on the pavements and on the sonorous bridges, the bells on the harness of the beasts of burden, the gongs of the beggars, the cadenced cries of the coolies, and the confused noises coming up from the canal, form a strange harmony, unlike the sounds of any other cities. All great cities have a voice of their own. In London it is like the surge of the rising tide, at Edo, it is like the murmur of a stream. As wave follows wave, so do generations succeed each other. That which I have under my eyes is passing away and disappearing, carrying with it all that its ancestors bequeathed to it, objects of worship, ancient costumes, old arms, laws dated from centuries, all these will soon be only a tradition to the new Japanese society that is forming itself in the school of the West.

The Sumida-*gawa* is the principal artery of Edo. The harbour at the mouth of the great river occupies the entire space between the small island of Ishikawa and the large triangular island that makes part of the district of Nihonbashi. Above the canal of this name the Eitai extends from the regions of the north-east of the triangle to the western bank of the district of Fukagawa. On both sides the population is essentially plebeian. With the exception of some *yashiki* of the second and third class, the houses of fishermen, mariners, and small shopkeepers form these quarters. The bridge, the squares, and the neighboring streets are constantly crowded with people of the lower classes, who have apparently no other object than recreation. The children play on the bridge and in the streets without any fear of being molested by the passers by. No less than four gigantic bridges span the banks of the Sumida-*gawa*, with intervals between them of about twenty minutes' walk. The squares on which they debouch, on the Honjo side as well as on that of Edo, are almost all equally spacious.

Ascending the river on the north of Edo we first come to the great bridge Ōgawa-*bashi*, so named because it is the largest of the four, the third and fourth bridges, Ryōgoku and Azuma, are very nearly as spacious, above the Azuma-*bashi* the river takes the name of Sumida-*gawa*. These limpid waters form the extreme limit of the quarters north of the citadel. A single bridge, with sixteen arches, called the Bridge of the Ōshū Kaidō, or the Northern Road, places the whole of this portion of the city in communication with the fields, the villages, and the rustic teahouses of the northern suburb, which abounds in fertile fields and charming views, and is the fautorite scene of parties of pleasure.

If the inhabitant of Edo is proud of his good city, he is additionally proud of the magnificent suburb called Yanaka, for he is susceptible alike to the charms of nature and the pleasures of society, and loves the cool retreats on the banks of the Sumida River as well as the crowded quays of the city. There are three things to which the Japanese refuses his sympathy. First, that perfidious element the sea, which he abandons to the fishermen, the boatmen, and the garrison of the six detached forts, secondly, the cold solitude of the monasteries. And thirdly, the formidable enclosure of the citadel and the Daimyōkōji. He keeps as far away from all these as his business will permit, and such pleasure as he takes in the city itself he seeks from a respectful distance from the seat of the government.

The Ryōgoku bridge may be regarded as the centre of the nocturnal merrymakings of the citizens and the *hatamoto*. This bridge, which is completely outside the commercial quarter of the city, places the Honjo in communication with the Asakusas, or two districts on the left bank, which contain the principal places of amusement in Edo. The river is not deep enough to float merchant junks at this height, but its surface is covered with hundreds of light boats, which can move about freely in all directions. During the fine nights in summer, rafts, laden with pyrotechnic devices, go up the stream and fling bouquets of stars towards the sky. Gondolas, ornamented with brilliantly colored lanterns, cross and recross from one bank to the other, while large barques, all decorated with lamps and banners, are slowly propelled, or lie still on the water, while their joyous crews are playing the guitar or singing. A crowd of bystanders lines the bridges and the quays, delighting in the animated and picturesque spectacle the river affords.

Edo, at these times, presents an almost identical picture of a Venetian festival, without omitting the Syrens, who are not wanting on the waters of the Sumida-*gawa* any more than on the Lagoons. On the other hand, we must be careful not to compare the great family boats of the Ryōgoku-*bashi* to the flower-laden barques of China. The former generally belong to respectable teahouses, and are let out by the hour, the proprietors of the teahouses furnishing their customers with refreshments and guitar players. They are only annexes of these teahouses, and occasionally of the little bamboo establishments built on the quays, and used by professional singers and musicians. The neighborhood of the bridges, far from injuring the effect of the productions of these humble artists, lends them an additional charm.

I have often passed many hours in genuine Japanese idleness, listening to the confused sounds of singing and instruments of music rising above the murmur of the crowds of foot passengers from the teahouse of the Ryōgoku-*bashi*.

The intervals of silence are broken by the distant noise of comers and goers on the wooden bridge. No roll of carriages, none of the discordant clamor of our European cities breaks the charm of our impressions. In Venice only, among European cities, can this same movement of the people, this same concert of steps, voices, sounds of music, be heard, without anything to trouble its peaceful cadence and its charming harmony. The Sumida-*gawa* reminds us of the Grand Canal, and the neighborhood of the bridges of Edo is, like the public squares of Venice, the rendezvous of the citizen population. The multitudes who meet each other there every evening cause no inconvenience whatever. For though Edo is par excellence a city of great dimensions, the Japanese people practise spontaneously that discipline of circulation our policemen have so much difficulty in establishing in our capitals. According to a Japanese saying, in order to be happy one must visit Edo. This extraordinary city contained, in 1858, one million eight hundred thousand inhabitants, and notwithstanding the fluctuations to which it is peculiarly subject, I believe the calculation then made of the number of the population, and their division into classes, may be taken to represent its actual condition with tolerable accuracy.

The southern portion of the city, in which the foreign legations are established, includes eight districts, all essentially plebeian. They contain a considerable agricultural population, devoted to the culture of kitchen-gardens, rice-grounds, and all the arable lands not yet invaded by dwellings. These districts are composed of a multitude of mean houses tenanted by fishermen, laborers, small artizans, retail shopkeepers, inferior officers, and low-class eating house keepers. A few lordly mansions break the uniformity of these wooden buildings by their long whitewashed walls. Monasteries and temples are scattered about everywhere, except in the two quarters built on the bay, Takanawa alone contains thirty.

The low streets and quays of Takanawa are filled from morning to night with a great concourse of people. The staple population of this quarter seems to live on taxes levied on all comers. Here tobacco is chopped and sold, there rice is packed and made into cakes, along the whole line dried fish, water melons, and an infinite variety of fruits and other cheap eatables are displayed on tables in the open air, or in innumerable restaurants. Everywhere there are coolies, porters, and boatmen offering their services. In the small side streets are stalls for the pack-horses and stabling for the oxen, who draw in the products of the surrounding country on the rustic carts which are the only wheeled vehicles in Edo.

At the doors of the teahouses of Takanawa, the singers, dancers, and wandering jugglers, who come to try their luck in the capital, make their first appearance. Among the former there exists a privileged class subject to police discipline. They may be recognized by their large flat hats pulled down on their foreheads, they always go about two by two, or four by four—two dancers accompanying the two musicians who play the *shamisen* and sing romantic songs. The fautorite tumblers of the Japanese streets are little boys, who, before they begin their tricks, hide their heads under a hood, surmounted by a tuft of cock's feathers, and wear a little scarlet mask representing a dog's muzzle. To the monotonous sound of their master's tambourine these poor children play their antics, representing the spectacle of a grotesque and really fantastic struggle between two animals with the heads of monsters and human limbs. The constant sound of gongs, and of the bells of the mendicant monks mingle with the deafening noises of the streets almost as frequently as at Kyoto. At Edo I perceived for the first time the monks were not shaven, and I inquired to what order they belonged. Our interpreter told me they were laymen merely, people of Edo making a trade or merchandise of devotion. Although they were all dressed in white, the sign of mourning and repentance, those who carried a long stick with a bell, some books in a basket, and a large white hat decorated at one side with a drawing of Fuji-*yama*, had just returned from accomplishing a pilgrimage to the holy mountain at the expense of public charity. The others, with a gong at the waist, a great black hat striped with yellow, and a heavy sack on their backs, were probably ruined shopkeepers, who had nothing better to do than to hawk about idols on commission for a monastery.

By following the great street that, beginning at the Tōkaidō, cuts obliquely the chain of hills on which the legations are built, and crossing the southern part of Takanawa in a straight line from north to south, we pass successively through three distinct zones of the social life of Edo. First, the southern zone, which I have just described, with its multitudes living in the open air and conducting all their business in the public street. Between the hills we find a sedentary population, devoted to various kinds of manual labour. Even their dwellings and their workshops may be distinguished from afar by their significant signs, here a board cut in the form of sandals or of a *kimono*, next to an enormous umbrella of wax-paper hanging above the shop; further on a quantity of straw hats of all dimensions suspended from the top of the roof and reaching the shop door. We look for a moment at the armorers and the burnishers engaged in repairing coats of mail, war fans, and sabres for the *samurai*, an old artizan perfectly naked squats on a mat, blowing the bellows of the forge with the great toe of the left foot, and hammering with his right hand an iron bar which he holds in his left. His son, also squatting in a corner, is putting the bars into the fire with a pair of pincers, and passing them to his father when reddened.

The chief of our escort bade us continue our march. By degrees the road began to be deserted. We were entering into the vast solitude of an agglomeration of seignorial residences. On our right extended the magnificent shade of the park belonging to the *daimyō* of Satsuma, on our left the boundary wall of the mansion of the *daimyō* of Arima. When we had turned the north-east corner we found ourselves before the principal front of the building, it stretches out parallel to a plantation of trees forming the bank of a limpid river which divides the Takanawa quarter from that of Akasaka.

One of our party, the Italian-British photographer Felice Beato, having made preparations to photograph this beautiful scene, two officers belonging to the *daimyō*'s household came to him and begged him to discontinue his operations. Our friend requested them to go and take the orders of their master on the subject, they went, but returned in a very few minutes, saying that the *daimyō* absolutely forbade that any view should be taken of his palace. Beato obeyed respectfully, and ordered the attendants to take away the machine. And the officers retired perfectly satisfied, without the slightest suspicion that during their temporary absence the operator had taken two negatives. The *yakunin* of our escort, who had been witnesses of this scene, unanimously applauded the success of our friend's trick, but when he told them that it was his intention to take a photograph of the cemetery of the *shōgun*, they in their turn opposed him, with a persistency that nothing could shake. We were even obliged to renounce the hope of entering the cemetery. We could perceive very distinctly the lofty red pagoda and the sombre groves of cypress, but we could only obtain leave to pass along the eastern side of the grove of Shiba—the name given to the holy place, and which occurs again in the complete designation of our own district Shiba-Takanawa.

We pass the river on an arched bridge, not far from the place where Henry Heusken was murdered. Leaving on our left a few houses of the Akasaka suburb which the fire had spared, we crossed a square, bounded on one side by an archery garden, and on the other by walls, behind which rise the plantations and roofs of the Zōjō-ji—a group of temples belonging to the great monastery, which has the honor of receiving the *shōgun* into their last resting places, there to abide under the combined protection of the two religions of the empire. Buddhism, it is true, is supreme in this place, where it possesses seventy sacred buildings, but among this number the ancient gods, Hachiman, Benten, and Inari, has each his own shrine. A shrine dedicated to the worship of the *kami* adorns the eastern avenue of Shiba on the side of Tōkaidō and the bay. In the same direction is the landing place of the *shōgun*, on the island of Hamagoten at the mouth of the Tamori River, which supplies the moats of the citadel.

Hamagoten forms a regular parallelogram, and is united by two bridges, which are closed to the public. I rowed almost all round it in our consular boat. The walls, the staircases, and the pavilions of the landing place, and the groves of trees surrounding it, are admirable in their grandeur, their simplicity, and their elegance. The river is bordered on both sides with great trees, which droop over its deep, pure waters.

We left the enclosure of Shiba, after we had reached its north-east limit. On that side is the palace of the high priest, and beneath it we were shown the avenue and the door exclusively reserved for the use of the *shōgun*. He passes through it but once a year, when he goes to make his obligatory devotions at the tombs of his ancestors. Every courtier, following his example, pays a ceremonious visit on one day of the year to his family burial ground.

We pursued our route towards the north. The district of Atago, which extends on our right as far as Hamagoten, is occupied by the residences of the *daimyō* and the great functionaries of the empire. On our left, fourteen little contiguous temples preseut themselves, those of Zōjō-*ji* extend to the foot of the hills of Atago-*yama*. A wide stream separates them from the public road, and each has its special bridge, door, and wall, surrounded by the chapels and habitations of the monks. At the back of the court is the shrine of the ablutions, the sacred grove, and the roof of the sanctuary. The sixth monastery is the exception. On crossing the threshold we saw a great flagged court, with a majestic *torii* of granite. When we passed in at the sacred door we found ourselves in the presence of two candelabra placed at the foot of an esplanade reached by a flight of steps. Then comes a second court bordered with fine trees, whose interlacing branches form arcades like that of a Gothic cathedral. Through their foliage we distinguished a wide stone staircase, the summit lost amid verdure.

We ascended the staircase, which consists of one hundred steps very regularly laid, to the top of the hill. On the right is another road, which crosses the wooded slopes, and is composed of a series of staircases, with flat terraces provided with *torii*.

A dilapidated oratory with two insignificant idols—one standing on a lotus, the other seated on a tortoise—with long covered galleries surrounding the teahouses, occupies the summit of Atago-*yama*. The young waitresses of the house hasten to serve us with refreshments, and we take a few minutes' rest before we approach the pavilions at the two extremities of the terrace.

At length the moment has come when we shall get a complete view of the great city. We begin at the southern pavilion, and we are at first dazzled by the extent and brilliancy of the picture. The sun is going down to the horizon in a cloudless sky, and the transparency of the atmosphere permits us to distinguish the forts on the luminous surface of the bay. But over the whole space that extends from the offing to the foot of the hill there is nothing to arrest one's gaze. It is an ocean of long streets, white walls, and grey roofs. The monotony of this picture is unbroken except by a few groups of trees with dark foliage, or a spire rising above the undulating lines of the innumerable houses.

In a neighboring quarter we observe a large hole cut through the streets, as if a bombshell had passed. It is the scene of a recent fire. At a little distance a sombre group of hills, consecrated to the sepulture of the *shōgun*, rises like a solitary island above a tumultuous sea.

The panorama seen from the northern pavilion is, if possible, more uniform. It includes the quarters inhabited by the nobility, and its limit on the horizon is the ramparts of the citadel.

The *daimyō yashiki*, or seignorial residences to which we improperly gave the name of palace, do not differ except by their dimensions. The most opulent and the simplest present the same type of architecture, the same character of simplicity. They are composed of a first enclosure of buildings reserved for the *daimyō*'s servants and men-at-arms. These buildings have only one storey above the ground floor, and form a long square, always surrounded by a ditch. A single roof covers them, a single wall protects them, and most frequently they have no other issue on the public road than this one door. The windows are numerous, low, and wide, regularly placed on two parallel lines, and furnished with wooden shutters. In the interior a more or less considerable number of houses divided into regular compartments, like the barracks of the *yakunin* at Benten, are placed diagonally all round, or on two sides at least, of the centre building. These are the quarters of the *daimyō*'s troops. A wide space separates them from a second railed enclosure, which contains the residency properly so called.

The dependencies of the palace face the military quarter. The principal building is surrounded by a verandah opening on an interior court, and on the garden with its tanks and its delicious shades. Such is the inviolable and silent asylum in which the proud *daimyō* shuts himself up in the bosom of his family during the six months of each year which the custom of the empire obliges him to pass in the capital.

We could form an idea of the dwellings of the Japanese nobility only from what might be discerned in a bird's-eye view of this quarter. No

European has ever crossed the threshold of a Japanese *yashiki*. The *shōgun*'s ministers, following the example of the nobility, have never permitted the foreign ambassadors to visit their dwellings, their personal relations are restricted to ceremonial audiences, which take place in certain buildings which belong to the administration, and correspond to the ministerial residences in our country. Among this number are the two marine schools on the shore of the bay, and the seat of the finance department, at the north-west extremity of Atago. Edifices of this kind have in general the same external appearance as the palaces of the *daimyō*.

The panorama seen from Atago-*yama* shows us only a fourth part of the great capital. On the north our view was bounded by the walls of the residences of the *shōgun*. We resolved to devote another day to the quarter which, with the citadel, forms the central portion of Edo.

The road we were about to follow resembled a mysterious labyrinth of stone, formed of the ramparts, the towers, and the palaces, behind which the power of the *shōgun* has entrenched itself for two centuries and a half. It is an imposing spectacle, but it creates a painful impression. The political order of things instituted in Japan by Tokugawa Ieyasu vaguely recalls the regime of the Venetian Republic under the rule of the Council of Ten. It has, if not all its grandeur, at least all its terrors—the sombre majesty of the chief of state, the impenetrable mystery of his government, the latent and continuous action of a system of espionage officially organized through all the branches of the administration, and bringing in its suite proscriptions, assassinations, and secret executions.

We must not push the comparison further. We vainly seek at Edo, in the vast extent of the citadel, any monument that deserves mention beside the marvellous edifices of the Piazza of St. Mark, artistic taste is completely wanting in the court of the *shōgun*. It has been relinquished to the people, with poetry, religion, social life, all those superfluous things that only clog the wheels of the governmental machine. From end to end of the administrative hierarchy, every functionary is assisted by a controller, the genius of the employer is exercised in doing nothing and saying nothing that can furnish matter for compromising reports. As to their private life, it is hidden, like that of the Japanese nobles in general, behind the walls of their domestic fortresses. While the streets of the town, composed of houses standing wide open on the public way, are constantly enlivened by a crowd of comers and goers of all ages and of both sexes, in the aristocratic quarters neither women nor children are to be seen, except indeed by stealth behind the window bars in the servants' quarters.

There are two societies in Edo—one, armed and privileged, lives in a state of magnificent imprisonment, in the vast citadel; the other, disarmed, and subject to the dominion of the first, seems to enjoy the advantages of liberty. But, in reality, an iron yoke weighs on the middle classes of the people of Edo. For every five heads of families, the shogunal administration sets up one as a magistrate over the other four. Iniquitous laws punish a whole family, a whole quarter, for the crime of one of its members. The properties, and even the lives, of the citizens, are secured by no legal guarantee. The extortions and the violence of the two-sworded men remain too frequently unpunished. The citizen finds compensation in the charms of the beautiful city. If the regime of the *shōguns* is severe, he remembers his subjects that the emperors were not always amiable, and that one of them delighted in exhibiting his skill as an archer by shooting down peasants who were forced to climb trees within easy reach of his arrows. The peoples of countries accustomed to despotism are puzzled to decide where their patience ought to stop.

A Japanese emperor, born under the constellation of the Dog, commanded that dogs were to be respected as sacred animals, that they should never be killed, and that at their death they should receive the honorus of sepulture. One of his subjects whose dog had died thought it right to inter the animal on one of the funeral hills. As he was going along, fatigued with the weight of the four-footed corpse, he ventured to remark to a friend who was accompanying him, that the emperor's decree appeared to him ridiculous. "Take care how you murmur," replied his comrade, "and recollect that our emperor might just as well have been born under the sign of the Horse."

The Sakurada quarter, which forms the first great line of defence of the citadel on the southern side, is surrounded by water on all sides, except the west, where it communicates with the Banjō quarter by the arsenal belonging to the *shōgun*. Ten bridges are thrown over the great ditches. The southern bridges have fortified gates, behind which the road makes a bend, which exposes it to the fire from the ramparts, and from the guns mounted in the interior.

A strong detachment of the *shōgun*'s troops occupies the guard house adjoining the gate through which we pass. The common soldiers are men from the mountains of Hakone, who are discharged after two or three years' service. Their uniform is made of blue cotton, and consists of tight trousers, and a shirt like that of the Garibaldian Volunteers, but crossed by white bands on the shoulders. They wear cotton socks, and leather soles fastened by sandals, also a belt, from which hangs a large sabre with a lacquer scabbard. A pointed hat of lacquered cardboard completes their costume, but they only wear it when mounting guard, or on parade.

The guns of the Japanese army are all percussion, with varied calibre and construction. I saw four different kinds in the racks of the barracks at Benten, into which a *yakunin* took me. He first showed me a Dutch model, then an arm of inferior quality, made at Edo, then an American gun, and finally the Minié rifle whose use was being taught by a young officer to a picket of soldiers in the courtyard. I remarked that this officer used the Dutch language. I asked him to come home with me, that I might show him my fowling piece and a Swiss carbie. Half a dozen of his comrades also accepted my invitation.

I have more than once been present at assaults of arms by the *yakunin*. The champions salute each other before attacking. The one who is on guard frequently kneels on the ground, to parry his adversary's blows more successfully. Each pass is accompanied by theatrical poses and expressive gestures, each blow provokes passionate exclamations on the part of both. Then the judges intervene and deliver their verdict. In the intervals the combatants drink tea, after which they recommence with great spirit. There is even a fencing school for the use of the Japanese ladies. Their arm is a lance, with a bent blade, which may be compared to a Polish reaping hook. They carry it with the point towards the ground, and manoeuver regularly in a series of attitudes, poses, and harmonious movements, which would look remarkably well in a ballet. I was not allowed to enjoy this pretty spectacle long. I only caught a glimpse of it in passing before the half-open court. My *yakunin* immediately shut the door, assuring me that the customs of the country did not permit beholders.

The Japanese nobles display much luxury, and take great pride in their arms, especially in their swords, which are of unrivalled temper, and are generally adorned on the handle and scabbard with ornaments in carved and wrought metal of extraordinary richness. But the principal value of these arms consists in their antiquity and their celebrity. Every sword in the old families of the *daimyō* has its tradition and its history, whose worth is measured by the blood it has shed. A new sword must not remain intact in the hands of the man who has bought it, while waiting for an opportunity of dyeing it in human blood, the *samurai* who has become its happy possessor tries it on live animals, or, what is still better, on the corpses of executed criminals. The executioner gives them up to him on being authorized so to do by the proper functionary, and he fastens them to a cross in his courtyard, where he practises himself in cutting and hacking until he has acquired sufficient strength and address to cut two corpses, tied together, through the middle.

It is easy to imagine the aversion with which the arms of the West inspire these Japanese gentlemen, for whom the sword is at once an emblem of bravery and a title to nobility. When the son of a *samurai* is too little to carry arms at his belt, he is seen walking, with an attendant, or even an elder sister, following him respectfully, and holding in her right hand, by the middle of the scabbard, a sword suitable to the height of the diminutive personage. In another year or two fencing will become the principal occupation of his life.

The *shōgun* selected a number of his young *yakunin*, and sent them to Nagasaki to learn the use of firearms under the tuition of the Dutch officers. They were not very well received when they returned to the capital, and were quartered in the barracks for the purpose of instructing the new Japanese infantry. Their former comrades shouted "Treason! "and threw themselves on them with arms in their hands. There were victims on both sides. Nevertheless the decline of the sword is inevitable. Notwithstanding the traditional prestige with which the privileged caste still endeavour to surround it, notwithstanding the contempt in which it affects to hold the military innovations of the government, that democratic arm the musket has been introduced into Japan, and with it an incalculable social revolution has become a fact the representatives of the feudal regime resent bitterly but vainly.

The conduct of their chiefs has precipitated the catastrophe. Conspiracies in the palace and political assassinations multiply themselves at Edo with frightful rapidity. It is averred that not only several ministers of state, but two *shōguns*, have successively died violent deaths since the opening up of Japan. The same fate has befallen the chief minister Ii Naosuke, the governor of the young sovereign, who was assassinated in 1860. His *yashiki* is situated on a hill, in the southern portion of the Sakurada quarter, in front of the wide ditches and the high walls forming the exterior enclosure of the citadel. It overlooks, on the east and the south, the great squares and streets formed by some fifty of the nobles' residences.

It was in this princely neighborhood that, on the 24th of March, 1860, at eleven o'clock in the morning, the regent, carried in his palanquin, and coming out of the citadel by the Sakurada bridge, with an escort of four or five hundred men, was assailed by a band of seventeen *rōnin* in the spacious public road, parallel with the ditch in the direction of his own palace. On both sides the fighting was severe. Twenty soldiers of the escort fell at their posts, five conspirators perished with arms in their hands, two performed *seppuku*, four were made prisoners, the others escaped—among them the chief of the expedition, who carried away the regent's head under his cloak. Public rumor adds that the head was exposed in the chief place of the province, in which the *daimyō* of Mito, the instigator of the conspiracy, resides, and then at Kyoto, before the buildings of the Dairi (the imperial palace), and finally that the Regent's people found it one day in the garden of the palace, into which it had been thrown, over the wall, in the night.

The portions of Edo inhabited by the aristocracy are almost entirely devoid of buildings consecrated to public worship. There is not one temple or shrine in the whole of the *daimyō*'s quarter. Banjō and Suruga have each three temples, but they are of little importance. There are half a dozen in Sakurada, amongst which is the Sannō Hiei *jinja*, a celebrated shrine under the invocation of Sannō, "the King of the Mountain." Its title is one of the surnames of Emperor Jinmu. The shrine contains an altar consecrated to Kannon and is the venue of the Sannō *matsuri*. The buildings and the groves of the sacred place occupy a group of hills, which rise above the southern enclosure of Sakurada, with its vast basins of limpid water surrounded by trees and flowers, and its myriads of birds.

The political system of the *shōguns* did not disdain clerical support for their budding dynasty. But as Ieyasu and his successors had nothing to hope from the good will of the emperors, they conciliated the favor of the most influential sects of Buddhism by endowing monasteries and temples, which surpass the most sumptuous sacred edifices of Kyoto. The munificence of the *shōguns* with regard to Buddhism has, however, added nothing to the reverence professed at Edo for the ministers of that religion. It appears that, in all the diverse classes of society in the capital, the position of the monks is analogons to that of the priests of the Greek Church when the latter come into contact with the nobles, the traders, or the serfs.

The Shintō priests worship are in a still less enviable condition, because their existence is hardly noticed. It is true that the representatives of the emperor at the court of the *shōgun*, and some provincial noblemen, honor them by their patronage, but the generality of the feudal nobility in residence at Edo stand entirely aloof from what is being done around them, in matters of religion as well as in everything else. They would prefer to pay a chaplain in the house rather than contribute to the support of any public worship whatever. The only thing they will do for the ancient national religion is to authorize the *kami* priests to send their collectors once a year to the aristocratic quarters. The priests, on their side, considering that it would be advisable to stimulate the charity of the higher classes by the attraction of some pious jugglery, have created two classes of collectors. The first, who go about in all seasons by order and at a fixed price, is composed of fortune-telling priestesses dressed in white surplices, with a holy wand made of paper in the left hand, and in the right a bunch of pebbles, they accompany their prophecies wath a kind of rhythmical dance, to which an attendant dressed in a Kyoto cap marks time by beating a large drum.

The second class of collectors go out only at the new year and pay general visits. The presents made on this occasion are voluntary. The persons charged with this office are the principal attendants of the *kami* temples, each of whom is followed by his own special attendant. The leader is dressed after the fashion of the ancient priests of the court of the emperor, with a lacquered cap, a great sword, and padded trousers, and he holds in his right hand a classic fan of cedar wood. His attendant, who is disguised as an attendant from Kyoto, carries a small tambourine, and a bag, destined to receive the gifts. Dances, comic songs, and burlesque pantomimes form the oratorical artifices of the two collectors. The buffooneries of the first are played up to by his attendant. Thus the sacred collection is effected from *yashiki* to *yashiki* in the midst of the laughter and applause of the noble feudal families, whose political existence rests entirely on the very religion they help to bring into contempt.

The immensity of the Japanese capital is exceedingly striking. Imagination and sight alike become weary of dwelling on this boundless agglomeration of human habitations, all bearing the same stamp of uniformity. Among our old cities in Europe each has a physiognomy proper to itself, though all are united by the charm of ancient memories and artistic achievements. At Edo, everything belongs to the same epoch, and is in the same style. Everything rests on one single fact, on the same political data—the foundation of the dynasty of the *shōguns*. Edo is a completely modern city, and seems to be waiting for its history and its monuments.

Even Edo castle, the residence of the *shōgun*, seen from a distance, is remarkable for its dimensions, its vast extent of terraces separated by enormous granite walls, its parks of magnificent trees, its moats covered with flocks of aquatic birds. In the interior the vast proportion of every-thing—walls, avenues of trees, canals, gates, guard and custom houses—is most impressive. The exquisite cleanliness of the squares and the avenues, the profound silence that reigns around, the noble and simple buildings of cedar with their marble basements, awaken those impressions of majesty, mystery, and fear which despotism demands for the maintenance of its prestige.

Here, as in the Japanese temples, we are forced to admire the sobriety of the means employed by the native architects for the realization of their most enduring conceptions. It is always from nature that they borrow their resources and ideas. The audience chamber of the *shōgun* possesses neither columns, statues, nor any kind of furniture. It is composed of a long line of rooms of great extent and height, separated from each other by moveable partitions which reach the ceiling. They are ranged in perspective, like the wings of a theater, and the back of the scene opens on the lawns and avenues of the immense parks.

Edo Commerce

The city, properly so called, extends to the east of the castle, from the bridge named Sen-*bashi*, which unites it to the Atago quarter towards the south, to that named Ōgawa-*bashi* at the limit of the northern quarter. It is composed of districts that lie exclusively in the direction of the south-west to the north-east. In the latter, the city stretches down to the Sumida-*gawa*; in the former, the banks and islands of the great river are for the most part occupied by public buildings or the residences of the nobles. Among them are a dozen *yashiki* of the *daimyō*, and some small *yashiki* belonging to the *hatamoto*. In the vicinity of the race course is the great temple of Nisi Hongan-*ji*, a few light batteries, and a government naval school.

The whole of the remaining space comprised between the citadel and the Sumida-*gawa* resembles an immense draught board, so completely symmetrical are all its sections, with their longitudinal streets regularly intersected by cross roads.

The district of Nihonbashi, which is in the heart of the city, contains five longitudinal and twenty-two transverse streets, cutting each other at right angles, and forming seventy-eight squares of houses almost identical with each other. It presents the figure of a long parallelogram, and navigable canals surround it on the four sides. Fifteen bridges communicate with the adjacent quarters—two on the west, which span the great moat of the citadel, five on the east, five on the south, and three on the north.

The Bridge of Nihon-*bashi*, on the north, which gives its name to the quarter is held to be the geometrical centre of Japan, from which all the geographical distances of the empire are measured. It is also at Nihonbashi that the Tōkaidō commences. Starting from the suburb of Shinagawa, it crosses the quarters of Takanawa, Atago, Kyōbashi, and Nihonbashi. At the extremity of the latter, a central bridge forms the limit between this great political, military, and commercial artery of the southern empire, and another, no less important, which stretches to the north. Beynd them lies the Ōshū Kaidō. It ends at the northern point of Japan, from where we cross the Tsugaru Strait in order to reach Hakodate, on the island of Hokkaido.

Although they have a completely homogeneous character, the city quarters do not convey such an impression of pompous monotony as the *yashiki* of the court and the feudal nobility. The citizens' houses, like the *yashiki*, preserve the type of architecture proper to them, they are simply wooden constructions, having but one storey above the basement, generally enclosed within an open gallery, their low roofs are made of slate-colored tiles, and ornamented with moldings in gypsum at the two ends. But if the frame be uniform, the pictures which it displays are of charming variety, oddity, and ingenuity.

At the upper end of the street of Nihonbashi we come on a barber's shop, in which two or three citizens, in the simplest apparel, are making their morning toilet. Seated on a stool, they gravely hold in the left hand a lacquered tray, destined to receive the soapsuds. The barbers, free from all clothing that could trammel the freedom of their movements, lean sometimes to the right and sometimes to the left of their customers' heads, over which they pass both the hand and the razor, like antique sculptors. I need hardly add that the illusion ceases when, holding between their teeth a long silken cord, they roll it round and tie it at each end, leaving the pudding-like ball that forms the Japanese headdress.

At a little distance we find a shoemaker's shop. It is adorned with innumerable wooden soles and numberless wooden sandals, which hang from the roof by long ropes of the same material. The shoemaker, squatting on his shelf, reminds me of the native idol to whom the beggars make presents of sandals. Many persons of both sexes stop before the shopfront, examining or trying on the merchandise, exchanging some amicable phrase with the shoemaker, and, without disturbing him from his quietude, lay the price at his feet. The accounts, so far as I could see, were kept in *zeni*— little pieces of iron, of which twenty make up a *tenpō*, or bit of copper money, worth fifteen centimes. The *zeni*, like Chinese cash, have a small square hole in the centre and are strung on a cord and hang from the girdle.

Next to the shoemaker's came the shop of a dealer in edible seaweed, which forms one of the principal articles of export trade between Japan and China. This seaweed is called *kombu*, and is found in great floating masses in all the bays of the insular empire. When the sea is calm, its rich golden purple and olive tints are distinctly seen through the still surface of the blue water. By means of a boatman's hook the fishermen draw it through the sea like an immense net, load their boats with it, and clean it carefully, collecting the little shells that cling to it in immense numbers. When the cargo has been landed, it is dried in the sun, and then formed into bundles tied with bands of straw, or in small parcels wrapped up in paper. The former are for export, and are sold by weight to the junks, the others are sold by the packet for a few *zeni*, and are to be bought either in the market or the eating houses.

At Edo there is an immense consumption of shellfish, the dealer fills his tubs, in which he shakes and turns them about with long bamboo sticks, after which he sets forth, crying his wares. Sea leeches, and all sorts of little molluscs, the trepang, and the whole class of radiates are sold in a dry state. They are eaten fried, and most frequently cut into pieces mingled with rice. One sort of fish, very thin, long, and narrow, is simply dried in the sun, and eaten without any further cooking. Oysters are abundant, but coarse. The Japanese have no method of opening them except by breaking the upper valve with a stone.

Uraga supports the whole empire with dried oysters, belonging to the large kind called *awabi*, the *shōgun* is said to have the monopoly of this trade.

Although the Japanese profess, from an aesthetic point of view, a profound disgust for shellfish, they do not seem to disdain them when they are fried and laid out on herbs and colored paper. I have remarked that delicacies of this sort have a great sale in the public markets.

The shops of the grain dealers at Edo are very interesting, from the immense quantity and the infinite variety of the products, the diversity of their forms and colors, and the art with which they are ranged on the shelves. But surprise and admiration succeed to curiosity when we perceive that on each of the parcels already done up in paper, on each of the bags ready to be delivered, is a colored drawing of the plants themselves, together with the name of the grain. This drawing is often a little masterpiece, which might figure in an album of the flora of Japan. Presently we see the painter and the workshop. The painter is a young girl, who lies at full length on mats covered with flowers and sheets of paper, and works incessantly in this singular attitude.

As we approach the central bridge of the commercial city the crowd increases, and on both sides of the street shops give place to popular restaurants, and confectioners, where cakes, rice, and millet are sold, and where hot tea and *sake* may be purchased.

We are close to the great fish market. The canal is covered with fishing boats, either discharging their cargo of both sea and river fish—great fish of the ocean currents that come down from the Pole, and those of the equatorial stream, tortoises and mussels from the bays of Japan, hideous jellyfish and fantastic crustacea. In this place Phillip Franz von Siebold reckoned seventy different kinds of fish, crabs, and molluscs, and twenty-six sorts of mussels and other shellfish.

Fish sheds, roughly put up near the landing place, are besieged by buyers. In the middle of the tumultuous crowd we see strong arms lifting full baskets and emptying them into the lacquered cases of the coolies. From time to time the crowd has to open, to give passage to two coolies laden with a dolphin, a shark, or a porpoise, suspended by ropes on a bamboo pole, which they carry on their shoulders. The Japanese boil the flesh of all these animals, and salt the whole blubber.

One of the strangest pictures in the environs of Nihonbashi is a group of shark and whale sellers, wholesale and retail. The stature, the dress, and the gestures of these personages, their fantastic equipment, the dimensions of the huge knives which they plunge into the sides of the sea monsters, suggest the prodigious exercise of human strength and employment of the resources of nature, which can alone suffice for the supply of the great city.

At the southern extremity of Nihonbashi, a barrier encloses several pillars covered with notices painted on white wood. And, a little further on, we find a pavilion raised on a granite platform, and containing a quantity of printed notices. This is the Kōkōsatsu of Edo, from where the ancient laws which are still in use are explained, and the daily ordinances of the shogunal police are announced.

Close by is a *yakunin* guard house and a post of the flying brigade. Wooden tubs and jars, filled with water and ranged in pyramids, are placed at intervals on the thresholds of the warehouses, and on the edge of the public pathways. These precautionary measures are taken in all the populous streets of Edo, and generally in ail Japanese cities. Reservoirs of water occupy the upper galleries and roofs of the houses. Long and strong ladders are planted against the great wooden buildings, such as temples and pagodas. Stores, known in the commercial language of the Far East under the name of godowns, are said to be fireproof. They are multiplied as much as possible in the wooden quarters, so as to present numerous obstacles to the spread of fire. These square, high buildings are constructed of stone, and covered outside with a thick layer of whitewash. Their doors and shutters are of iron, and from the four walls great hooks stick out, from which wet mats and mattresses may be hung when there is imminent danger.

The godowns, the ladders, and the tubs do not contribute to the embellishment of the capital. In this, as in other details of Japanese life, the beautiful is sacrificed to the useful, and visitors must just make the best of the charming accidental views that occur in the city. Its religious buildings would render it exceedingly beautiful, were not its chief sites occupied by the endless lines of warehouses.

Pursuing our route from street to street, we look into the interior of the houses, with hardly any interruption from the sliding panels, and see the picturesque groups of men, women, and children squatting round their humble dinners. The straw tablecloth is laid on the mats which cover the floor, in the centre is a large wooden bowl containing rice, which forms the principal food of every class of Japanese society. Each guest attacks the common dish, and takes out enough to pile up a great china cup, from which they eat without the aid of the sticks that serve for a fork, except just for the last few mouthfuls, to which they add a scrap of fish, crab, or fowl, taken from the numerous plates that surround the centre bowl. These viands are seasoned with sea salt, pepper, and soy—a very strong sauce made from black beans by a process of fermentation, eggs, soft and hard, fresh or preserved, boiled vegetables, such as turnips, carrots, and sweet potatoes, slices of young twigs of bamboo, or a salad of lotus bulbs, complete the bill of fare of a Japanese citizen's dinner.

The meal is invariably accompanied by tea and *sake*, and these two beverages are ordinarily drunk hot, without any other liquid, and without sugar. The teapots that contain them stand on a brasier shaped like a casket, it is a little larger than another corresponding article of furniture called a *tabako-bon*, on which coal, a pipe rack, and a supply of tobacco are placed.

I have never examined the pretty utensils used at a Japanese table—the bowls, cups, saucers, boxes, lacquered trays, vases of porcelain, jugs and teapots in glazed earthenware—nor have I ever contemplated the people while eating, seen the grace of their movements, and watched the dexterity of their delicate little hands, without fancying I was looking on at a number of grown-up children playing at housekeeping, and eating rather for their amusement than because they were hungry.

Maladies resulting from excess or from unwholesome diet are generally unknown, but the immoderate use of their national beverage sometimes produces grave results. I have seen more than one case of delirium tremens.

The ravages caused by dysentery and cholera in certain parts of Japan, especially at Edo, will cause no surprise to the European resident, who has seen how greedily children and the lower classes of the people devour water-melons, limes, Siam oranges, and all sorts of fruits at the beginning of the autumn, before they are fully ripe.

Japanese houses are rarely supplied with really wholesome water, because, even at Edo, where springs are abundant, they use only cisterns, though it would be easy to establish fountains in every quarter in the town. The inconvenience and danger of this state of things are, however, reduced by the fact that the Japanese are in the habit of using hot drinks in all seasons.

Their popular hygiene demands hot baths, which they take every day. This extreme cleanliness, the salubrity of their climate, and the excellent qualities of their diet, aid in making the Japanese one of the healthiest and one of the most robust of peoples. There are very few of them who do not suffer from diseases of the skin, and from chronic and incurable maladies, which are not to be traced to their natural conditions. This great misfortune dates from the epoch at which the government of the *shōgun* authorized the foundation and officially protected the development of prostitution, whose fatal consequences sap the entire edifice of society.

There are a great number of physicians in Japan, principally at Edo. Those who are attached to the court of the *shōgun* belong to the *hatamoto* class, carry two swords, shave the head, and occupy a more or less elevated rank according as they belong to either category of functionaries. The first, which is necessarily very limited, comprises the physicians of the *shōgun*'s household; they do not practise outside the palace. The second category are the officers of health who accompany the army in time of war, and who, when they are not on service, practise among the families of their own relations. Both one and the other are nominated by the *shōgun* or his government.

The members of the medical body who are neither functionaries nor officers, that is to say, who practise as physicians of the third class, belong to the bourgeoisie. They have generally been educated at the University of Kyoto or that of Edo. But some, who belong to families where the medical profession has been followed from father to son, have received an education under the paternal roof.

As no examinations are required for the practice of medicine, each man enters the profession when he pleases, and practises according to his own fancy, some healing by the routine of the native empirics, others treating their patients according to the rules of Chinese science, a third claiming to be adepts in Dutch medicine. But in reality they have actually neither method nor system. University studies in Japan are exceedingly superficial. It cannot be otherwise in a country where no one possesses the preparatory knowledge, which is taken for granted on entering on a university course. This state of things can only be reformed by frequent contact with Europeans. The people, however, do not care about it. All they want is to have a number of doctors at their disposal, to be treated and physicked rather on these conjoint methods than on the best, supposing it to exist. The prefer to find in their physicians pleasant servants, who will not contradict the notions of their patients, and who scrupulously justify the confidence with which their profession is honored. This obliges them to adopt a certain demeanor that impresses the public, and sets them apart from the rest of society.

Japanese medical practitioners may be easily recognized by their dress, by their methodical demeanor, and some other peculiarities, which vary according to the fancy of these grave personages. I have seen one whose head was shaved like that of a monk, or of an imperial doctor, though he certainly belonged to a physician of the third class. I have seen others wearing their hair long and plaited, the ends coiled on their neck, and others with a profuse beard. Their middle class extraction not permitting them to wear two swords, they wear one, passed through the folds of their girdle. But it is always a very small one, and generally carefully wrapped up in crape or velvet. Certain members of the faculty take care never to show themselves in public without an attendant carrying their instrument case and medicines.

The third class command public esteem and enjoy uncontested respect. I have heard it said, that when they are sent for to aristocratic houses they are paid by those sentiments rather than in *ichibu*. It is well known that the greater number—even those who possess an extensive connection—can hardly live, for the citizens' families generally find at the end of the year, when they have met their indispensable expenses—housekeeping, annual festivals, the theater, the baths, the monks, and the parties of pleasure—that they have very little left to give to the doctor.

The latter, on his side, accepts the situation with philosophy, and it must be added to his credit, that he is generally a truly disinterested person. Many possess real scientific zeal, and a taste for the observation of nature that might produce remarkable results if these qualities rested on a solid basis or sufficient preparatory instruction. There is no doubt that the medical fraternity is one of the most energetic agents of progress and civilization in Japan. The fraternity is one of a corporation of arts and professions that enjoys an official constitution and certain privileges. It was placed by the emperor under the invocation of a holy patron, and is evidently of great antiquity. We learn from the imperial annals of Kyoto that the first Japanese pharmacy was founded in 730, that in the year 808 medical science was enriched by a collection of recipes published in one hundred volumes by the Heian physiscian Izumu Hirosada, and that the year 825 endowed the empire with its first hospital.

For a long time Japan was tributary to China in all that concerns medical science, as well as in the other branches of human knowledge. The celestial empire supplied it with works on anatomy and botanical treatises, books and recipes, as well as professors, medical practitioners, and ready-made medicines for curing an infinity of ailments. In the second half of the eleventh century, the Chinese merchant Wangman made a fortune by selling medicines and parrots in Japan.

At that time the resources of art were added to the secrets of magic. In the present day the successors of the early practitioners in this line carry about *kimono* covered with cabalistic signs through the towns and villages. These *kimono*, placed at an opportune moment on the body of a patient, have the power of recalling a dead man to life. The monks, on their side, know prayers of a sacramental kind that stop bleeding, heal wounds, exorcise insects, cure burns, and counteract the evil eye, in the case of men and animals.

Two great events, of which one occurred at the beginning and the other at the end of the seventeenth century, prevented the scientific labours of the medical fraternity from being shrouded by degrees in the great darkness of Buddhist superstition. The first was the arrival of the Dutch, who received their letters of franchise and inaugurated their factory at Hirado under the direction of the superintendent, Jacques Specx, in the year 1609. And the second was the foundation of the University of Edo, which took place in the reign of the thirty-sixth *shōgun*, Tokugawa Tsunayoshi, the fourth successor to Ieyasu, in 1690.

Carl Peter Thunberg recounts how, towards the middle of the following century, being at Edo as attache to the biennial embassy from the Dutch superintendent of Deshima, he obtained permission from the *shōgun* to receive a visit from five physicians and two astronomers attached to the court. He had long conversations with them, and convinced himself from the observations of the former that they had derived their knowledge of natural history, physics, medicine and surgery, not only from the traditional Chinese sources, but from Dutch works too. At a later date, the physicians of the factory, having been authorized to take pupils, strove, with great zeal and devotion, to impart to them the medical science of the West.

If the judgment of civilized peoples were not distorted by the manner in which they are taught history—if they had learned that science has its honorus as well as war—they would look with admiration on the peaceful conquests that have been made in the empire of Japan, to the advantage of the whole world, by the physicians of the factory at Deshima since the time of Kaempfer to the present day.

Honjo, properly so called, answers in some respects to the industrial quarters of our great cities. It contains manufactories of tiles and of coarse pottery, kitchen utensils in iron, paper factories, and workshops for the cleaning and preparation of cotton, for the weaving of cotton and silk fabrics, dyeing vats, weavers' shops, basket makers, and mat plaiters.

Japanese industry has not yet utilized machinery. There are, indeed, iron foundries, in which the bellows are moved by an hydraulic wheel, over which the water is directed by tubes of bamboo. The combustible material is composed of charcoal and coal, the former of excellent quality. Women have their share in every kind of industry. No great manufactories exist in Japan, neither the occupation nor the population of our factories is represented there. The working classes labour in their own houses, interrupting their toil by eating when they are hungry, and resting when it pleases them. In a group of six artizans of both sexes, we always find one or two smoking their pipes and enlivening their comrades by their gay talk. Thus from generation to generation an instinct of sociability is transmitted, and good humor and repartee generally characterize the lower classes of the capital.

At Edo, as in all other capitals through which a river runs, the population of the lower bank and that of the centre of the city present entirely different features. Honjo has not the continual movement, the imposing mass of residences within the citadel, nor the animation of places reserved for the pleasures of the crowd in the northern quarter. Still, we find in it commerce, industry, temples, palaces, and places of public amusement, but under quite special conditions. Some of the great merchants of Japan live in Honjo, while their counting houses are in the quarters of Kyōbashi, or Nihonbashi, after the fashion of the great merchants of Rotterdam, who have their houses at Verkade, and their counting houses among the stores of Wijnstraat.

The relative tranquillity of the left bank, and the facility with which ground can be obtained there, have been favorable to the establishment of numerous monasteries. Some of them possess very large temples. Among the twenty or thirty temples of the Fukagawa quarter, the ancient national worship of Shintō is principally represented by the two celebrated temple of Tenmangu and Hachiman: and the Buddhist worship by the temple of Sanjūsan Gendō. In Honjo, where there are forty temples of different denominations, the Rakan-*ji*, or the Tennōzan Gohyaku Rakan-*ji*, the Temple of Five Hundred Arhats, consecrated to the memory of arhats and other illustrious Buddhist saints, are chiefly distinguished. Formerly this venerable army, entirely composed of wooden statues, larger than life and faded in color, was displayed on the galleries of the nave, the choir and the side chapels of the holy place, or the right and left of a colossal idol of Buddha. An earthquake flung its ranks into confusion. The mutilated victims were collected in the barns in the neighborhood, and the devastated temple has not yet been repaired and restored for the purpose of worship.

At a little distance, another monastery has founded its reputation on a less fragile basis than the images of the defunct heroes of asceticism and contemplation. Twice a year it engages the services of the chief wrestlers of Edo for a series of public representations, and this pious speculation never fails to attract an immense crowd belonging to all classes of society. Every monastery has its peculiarity. For instance, the avenue of the monastery of Honjo is guarded by half a dozen statues of pigs, mounted on granite pedestals. Public opinion admits, without difficulty and by silent consent, anything which the monks please to imagine may lend a novel attraction to the exercise of devotion.

A certain number of families of the old nobility have made of Honjo a sort of St. Germain, where they live in profound seclusion, far from the noise of the city, and from all contact with the court and the government functionaries. In addition to the larger industries I have enumerated, we find in Honjo important manufactories of silk, materials, and porcelain utensils, household furniture, and toilet ornaments of lacquered wood, as well as great workshops of sculpture, cabinet making, and wood-inlaying. I never saw marble works anywhere, though there are quarries in the mountains of the interior. All the candelabra and the pillars of the *torii* are granite, as are also the candelabra of the holy places, the tombs, statuettes, and funeral stones, as well as the Buddha, the sacred tortoises, and foxes, are made of a very fine kind of earthenware. Sculptors in wood make domestic altars with very rich panels, elegant reliquaries and coffins in the form of *mikoshi*, elephants' heads, monstrous chimeras for the adornment of the temple roofs, wood carvings and mosaics, representing cranes, geese, bats, and mythological animals, the moon half-veiled by a cloud, branches of cedars, pines, bamboos, and palms.

The idols, which are generally gigantic, come from the workshops of Edo, and are frequently surrounded by a golden nimbus, and painted in very bright colors—the guardians of heaven, for example, in vermilion, Tengu in indigo, the foxes are white, brown, or gilded, and generally have a golden key in their mouths. Several interesting branches of industry are connected with the work of the sculptors. The panels of the moveable partitions are ornamented with drawings in Chinese ink, traced by a few strokes of the brush, or with groups of trees and flowers, brilliantly colored with paintings of birds famous for the richness of their plumage. All this is done in the manufactory, but by hand. Nothing is printed except the papers for wall-hangings or the woodwork.

The embroidresses, who make the screens that serve for blinds and shutters, work beautifully. They employ silk, and reproduce, according to the subjects, either the lustrous tissue of leaves, the velvet down of birds, the thick fur of quadrupeds, or the brilliant scales of fish. The silk plaiters add to the woodwork and the hangings of rooms a beautiful ornament composed of garlands and knots of various colors, headed by groups of flowers and birds. These delicate arts of embroidery and braiding are also applicable to the heavy materials brocaded in gold and silver, of which the court mantles and long trailing dresses are made. We also find crape and gauze of extreme fineness, adorned with needlework of the purest taste.

The *obi*, or girdle worn by all Japanese women, married and unmarried, with the exception of the ladies of the princely families, is that portion of female dress which presents the greatest variety according to the taste and fancy of the wearers. Sometimes the *obi* affects great simplicity—sometimes it is distinguished for richness of material and profusion of embroidery, it is generally wide enough to suffice at the same time for girdle and corset, it is wrapped round the body and tied behind the back in an elegant bow, in which the end is caught up. The result is a sort of wide floating knot, which falls squarely down on the hips, or a large loop, which hangs from the girdle with much elegance. A widow who has made up her mind not to marry again ties her *obi* in the front of her dress. Every woman, after her death is clad in her best costume, the *obi* is arranged after the fashion of a widow's, it is then tied as tight as possible in two knots.

It is not an easy thing to get admission to Japanese workshops, especially when one's escort consists of *yakunin*. Notwithstanding the promises of their masters, I was not permitted to witness the process of dyeing, to see the manufacture of rich silk materials, or any paper factory. On the other hand, I found the wholesale and retail shops quite accessible, and was even allowed to go into the back shops, which are by no means unworthy of a visit, because the Japanese merchant does not care about show. Far from putting his most valuable objects for sale in the front, he keeps them in reserve—a fact well known to amateurs, so that, in order to have an idea of the wealth, variety, and artistic merit of Japanese fabrics, it is necessary, not only to visit the trading streets of the natives, but to make friends with the shopkeepers, and come back again and again to the shops, until one has explored all their corners and recesses. This is the more indispensable as there is no bazaar in Japan, and every shop and workshop has its speciality.

There is, indeed, a small native bazaar, established under the name of "stores," in the ports open to Europeans. But these are only permanent exhibitions of samples, and offer no real opportunity for studying Japanese industry, which in some branches is but little developed—for instance, that of saddlery, which must necessarily remain so where religious prejudices shackle the trades of the tanner and the leatherworker. This circumstance obliges Japan to lie under obligations to foreign countries, especially since the *shōgun* and the *daimyō* have carried on a jealous rivalry in the reform of their artillery and cavalry. Germany supplies them with leather, Holland and France with saddles and horse-trappings, gloves, and belts. Trade in skins, which is so widely extended in China, has scarcely any existence in Japan.

The Mongols delight in wrapping themselves in furs, while the Japanese regard fur with repugnance. Neither the Chinese nor the Japanese preserve or prepare the skins of beasts for stuffing. The Chinese make artificial birds, whose bodies are modelled in wax, with real feathers gummed on one after the other with the most minute care. The Japanese employ nothing but silk in making images of their fautorite animals. They excel in reproducing, in miniature, cocks, hens, pheasants, ducks, cats, and little spaniels. They employ hair and natural feathers only in making dust-brushes, fly-brushes, and fans. These objects are sometimes very elegant, especially the fly-brushes and the fans of white feathers spotted in the middle with two or three little feathers of bright colors. The making of paint-brushes is carried to extreme perfection and cheapness, which is to be expected in a country in which this one kind of instrument is used for writing, drawing, and painting. The Japanese brushes are made of the hair of otters, weasels, and foxes. Those that are got from the principality of Satsuma are considered to be the best.

Silken cord plays a great part not only in the fabrication of horse-trappings, but for the fastenings of casques and cuirasses, in all military equipments, and civil costumes, for men as well as women, because our buttons, hooks, clasps, and *aiguillette* are perfectly unknown in native apparel. Coarse ropes and cables are made of Manilla cotton, and vegetable paper. The silken cords do great honor to the art of those who make them, those used for flying kites and falconry are very elegant. The strings of musical instruments are made of silk covered with varnish.

Window blinds are generally ornamented by drawings of flowers and birds very skilfully done. The fishermen's cloaks, and brooms, are made of fine strips of palm bark. Birdcatchers and sellers of poultry use bamboo cages, whose forms vary from the common type of the beehive and the covered basket, to beautiful models of country pavilions and garden houses. We also noticed tall turrets made of bamboo trellis, in which the restaurateurs hang their finest specimens of game, such as the wild boar, the deer, and the black bear of Hokkaido. Animals famed for their malignity are not shown so much honor. The fox, extended on the stall, holds the knife with which he is about to be cut up in his mouth. And the monkey, suspended by his four paws to the lintel of the door, is exposed to the ridicule of the street children, who laugh at his grinning red face.

The artizan of Edo is a true artist. If we except the conventional style that he retains in his reproductions of the human figure, and excuse the insufficiency of his studies in perspective, we can have nothing but praise to bestow on him. His works are distinguished from those of Kyoto by simplicity of form, severity of line, sobriety of ornament, and exquisite feeling for nature in all the subjects of decoration he borrows from the vegetable or animal kingdom. In such subjects he delights. Flowers and birds inspire him with compositions full of truth, grace, and harmony, while the execution is equally admirable in the works of the artists of both capitals.

The Japanese do not understand the fabrication of panes of glass and of bottles. But they delight in making all sorts of little objects in glass—pipes, and water bowls, and long blue stems, little white cups at the bottom of which we see a tiny red crab, rising to the surface according as the cup becomes full of liquid. And little balls half filled with colored water, ornaments much used by the women in their headdresses.

At Edo I was shown some attempts at painting on glass, and at enamel-work which denoted more goodwill than science. But among a number of native curiosities that are really original, are little balls of stone pierced and cut in facets and enriched with enamel arabesques. These are extensively bought by foreigners for necklaces, and used in Edo itself for making rosaries. For the latter purpose they are strung on silk.

Mother-of-pearl competes with enamel in certain miniatures that are applied on metal. The gilders' art consists entirely in the application of their leaves of gold to such things as are thought worthy of this decoration, for instance, the nimbus round the heads of saints in the Buddhist temples, the frames of theater scenes, the sculptures of altar pieces, the lances from which the military standards are displayed, and the leaves of screens of the very first style. Among the latter we find exquisite specimens of drawings in Chinese ink representing hunting scenes, and horses, all done with two brushes and a single line on a gold background.

The stories coming to us from former embassies singularly exaggerate the decorative richness of the palaces of the emperor and *shōgun*. The truth is that there is no royal residence in Europe which does not represent a greater intrinsic value than the imperial palaces of Kyoto and Edo. Strictly speaking there arc neither goldsmiths nor jewellers in Japan. The serpentine, the malachite, the amethyst, the topaz, are all found in the country, but no one, not even the most elegant among the women, wears jewelled ornaments, Their only luxury after that of fabrics consists in loading the heavy edifice of their headdress with large pins of shell or metal, ornamented with small pictures on emblematic subjects. The lapidaries of Edo have nothing to do except to cut rock crystal, of which very fine specimens arc brought to Europe. These are exquisitely polished, and cut either round or in facets, but they cost an exorbitant price.

The closest approach to goldsmith's work is found in the ornamentation of the arms of the *yakunin*, which are sometimes marvels of carving, and of the mingling of metals. Gold, silver, steel, copper, brass, and a composition known as Sawa metal, are used for this purpose, and also for paper weights, clasps, locks, portfolios, and rulers. Of all the cities of Japan, Edo can boast of the most skilful workers in metals. Numbers of depots in the city are among the most interesting of the native curiosities.

I need not dwell on the perfection of their porcelain, second only to which are their masterpieces in brass and their works in lacquered wood. Such is the talent with which the native workman utilizes the incomparable varnish of Japan, such is their skill in combining its effects with the processes of their decorative art, that articles of furniture whose material is held of no value at all rival in brilliancy—we might almost say substance—those which in our country are made of marble and precious metals.

In the interior decoration of cabinets, boxes, and coffers, brown lacquer spangled with gold is extensively used. But for the exterior the lacquer is generally of one clear red, brown, or black, adorned with drawings of two or three colors, or with gold leaf, with or without relief. There is seldom anything in the form, in the drawing, or in the ornamentation that cannot sustain criticism by the most cultivated taste. If the cabinets are sometimes too heavily laden with incrustations of porcelain and mother-of-pearl, silver, and even gold, we may be quite sure that the native workmen have been obliged to study the caprices of foreign purchasers, who want to find in the Japan market something of the heavy splendor of the Chinese shops.

An indispensable ceremonial in all Japanese banquets is the serving of *sake*. This beverage is brought in solemnly in large lacquered jars or in cans of metal. The large or small cups from which it is drunk are made of fine red lacquer, and ornamented with fantastic designs, with gold leaf or rich paintings, covered with a transparent glaze. Some of these beautiful cups represent the most celebrated landscapes in Japan, or the most remarkable towns situated between the two capitals. There are even some of a still more sumptuous order formed of the nautilus in mother-of-pearl, the abalone, and other beautiful shells ornamented with silver filigree.

Asakusa

Over one hundred monasteries, each composed of a more or less considerable number of buildings, such as monasteries, temples, pagodas, shrines, teahouses, and shops, form the central division of the quarter of Asakusa. The greatest and most famous is that of Kannon, a Buddhist divinity, to whom is attributed the magical power of intercession between heaven and earth. The celebrity of this monastery completely eclipses all the other holy places of the neighborhood, so that in the language of the people the word Asakusa-*dera* is never used to designate any other temple than that of Kannon in the quarter of Asakusa.

At the southern extremity of the square, in which there is a permanent market of shrubs and flowers, stands a heavy portal adorned with colossal lanterns. Two of the guardians of heaven, wooden giants painted in vermilion, are posted on the right hand and on the left of the principal entrance, defending the passage, and levying on each pilgrim the traditional tribute of a pair of enormous straw sandals. Under their eyes, on the eve of each new year, a gratuitous distribution of paper amulets is made to the populace. The monks for the most part visit their clients on this day, and for a small consideration bring to their houses bits of the brush with which they distribute holy water. These scraps are fastened to the lintels of the door, and are believed to preserve the house from evil spirits.

The coolies, and laborers of all kinds, flock to Asakusa to have their share in the same privilege, because there they can obtain it without expense, though not without trouble. Two monks, perched at the risk of their lives on a platform composed of planks suspended by hooks halfway up the high columns of the doorway, are distributing an abundant provision of blessed papers. They take handfuls of them at intervals, and throw them into the air. The attendants standing on either side, provided with large palm leaf fans, make the amulets fly about and fall on the people like snow-flakes. Let him catch them who can. Soon the entire space presents a spectacle of extraordinary confusion, people pushing, elbowing, pursuing each other— some stretching out their arms in order to catch the morsels of paper in their flight, others bending, and even rolling themselves on the ground, in order to pick them up. Nevertheless, as the most fortunate and the most skilful retire when they have obtained their share, success becomes for their rivals a mere matter of patience, and no one is compelled to return home empty-handed.

Beyond this great gateway is a long, wide, paved street. It is intersected by cross-lanes, and occupied from one end to the other by booths for the sale of sacred objects, such as rosaries, wax candles, statues, perfumed vases, and domestic altars. Above and beyond the middle-class houses are oratories, small temples, and various curiosities, which warmly interest the pilgrims from the town and the country. Here is a Shintō shrine consecrated to the *kami* worship. There, surrounded by a bamboo railing, stands the venerable trunk of a cedar of unknown age. Further on, in an oratory hung with ex-votos, is a miraculous image. Beyond that comes a small aristocratic temple approached by an avenue of banners planted in the ground, each bearing the arms and the family names of some one of the illustrious personages who have honored this place by their visits. At the eastern extremity of the street, a hill surmounted by a temple rises above a little lake covered with waterlilies. The teahouses stretch out their long wooden galleries amid the leaves and flowers of the splendid aquatic plants. On the other side of the public road, a small monastery is half hidden by a cedar grove.

At length we reach the second gateway, which stands in the great square, almost surrounded by shops and by the booths of strolling actors. On the right, two huge sitting statues of brass, the heads crowned by the Buddhist nimbus, overlook the crowds from the height of the granite terrace. Two enormous guardians of heaven defend the second doorway, as their colleagues defend the first. From the galleries surrounding the upper storey of this building we can see the whole square, the high road, and, on the north, the first enclosure of the principal temple, which has numerous dependencies. Under the name of Asakusa-*dera* is in reality comprehended an agglomeration of from forty to fifty sacred buildings, including the sanctuary of Kannon-*sama*, the chief divinity and patron of the place, whose power of intercession is signified by an enormous statue, with thirty-six arms and one hundred hands, placed at the entrance of the temple. Under its protection are grouped the shrines of Sannō, the ruler of men, Daikoku, the god of riches, Benten, the goddess of harmony, Hachiman, the patron of warriors, in a word, the entire national mythology, not excepting the worship of the fox. This diabolical animal is worshipped, as well as his companion Inari, the patron of cereals, on the summit of a wooded hill, within the enclosure of the monastery. His little shrine, thickly hung with ex-votos, is reached by an avenue in which we pass innumerable *torii* painted vermilion. From the one to the other the distance is only that of a fox's jump, and they are hardly as tall as a man. The road is steep, winding, and impeded by the roots of the pines of the sacred grove. It is impossible to climb it, except with great care and by bending the head.

In that humble attitude we reach the esplanade of the holy place. There we must pass between two granite images representing the malicious divinity in a sitting posture, his tail turned up, his muzzle in the air, but his oblique eye watching every person who approaches the sanctuary. The faithful bow respectfully, make their ablutions, cast their pieces of money into the box, and kneel in prayer on the steps of the shrine.

Among the numerous buildings placed in the enclosure of Asakusa-*dera*, a pagoda of five storeys symbolizes the supremacy of Buddhism over other religions. The central building is an enormous quadrangular edifice—the body painted red, and the colossal roof covered with grey tiles. The basement only is in stone, and supports a spacious gallery raised some yards above the ground. In the interior of the temple, the ceiling rests on colonnades of red pillars, the walls of the nave are adorned with pictures on a golden ground. Framed images, statuettes, ex-votos, lacquered boards, with inscriptions in gold letters, are to be seen on all sides—on the columns, and on the panels of the side shrines.

One of the latter buildings contains a gallery of portraits of the most celebrated courtesans in Edo, as well as other pictures of a similar nature. Not only do the monks of Myōjin and the priests of the Sannō Hiei shrine invite courtesans to take a share in the periodical religious processions. But every year, in the enclosure of Shin-Yoshiwara, a fair takes place, accompanied by a grand parade, which is simply a public exhibition of the five thousand registered courtesans who inhabit this quarter. And the monks of Asakusa-*dera* have portraits of the queens of the festival taken on these occasions, and suspended in their sanctuary as if in a pantheon.

The choir of the temple, dark and smoked from the vapor of the incense, does not present any remarkable peculiarity, except that on the high altar, is the idol Kannon, symbolizing the mother of Buddha, behind a trellis of wirework, wearing a nimbus and seated on the sacred lotus. This mysterious combination excites little notice from the crowds of people who pass to and fro, and keep up a perpetual tumult in the nave, which is not spacious, and is separated from the choir by a lofty barrier of carved wood like a Gothic choir screen. In the choir the monks, laden with their heavy sacerdotal vestments, officiate to an accompaniment of gongs and tambourines. Some of the faithful merely throw iron money wrapped in a white paper at their feet from behind the barrier, others buy the candles the sacristan offers them. Before and after the hours of workship, a large covered box which, in front of the railing, communicates with the underground portion of the temple, receives the gifts of the visitors.

The solemn entry of the high priest into the choir makes an immediate diversion in the monotony of the service. This majestic personage wears a red cloak, with a pointed hood and a green silk stole over his white robe. He is followed by a young novice, who might be taken at first sight for a young girl, so effeminate are his face, complexion, and dress. His headdress is an elegant edifice of plaited hair, he wears loose white trousers, a white sash tied in wide bows, a short vest of green silk, with long hanging sleeves lined with white satin, he accompanies his master, step by step, to offer him, at the first sign he makes, a cup of tea contained in a portable vessel, the handle of which he holds in both hands.

On beholding the present ministers of the religion of Buddha, we cannot refrain from thinking rather sadly of the pious reformer whose disciples they claim to be.

The Buddhist pentalogue is conceived in these terms:

1. Thou shalt not kill.
2. Thou shalt not steal.
3. Thou shalt not commit fornication.
4. Thou shalt not lie.
5. Thou shalt abstain from all intoxicating liquor.

What has become of the ascetic purity of the Good Law in the hands of men who are plunged, for the most part, in the lowest degradation? What ironical destiny pursues the precepts of the great Shakyamuni in the midst of this temple, where art glorifies the corruption of morals, where incense burns before an idol who gives indulgences for every crime, where the industry of the monks is exercised in making money of the vices, as well as of the sanguinary passions, of the nobility, in imposing on the credulity of the people and fostering their profligacy?

The monastery of Asakusa is distinguished for the luxury and variety of the costumes of its monks, and for its immense personal staff, also for the theatrical pomp of its ceremonies. The most imposing is the general procession of the annual dedication that follows the feasts of the purification of the temple and its dependencies. The superiors of the convent have the head shaved and conform in all its details to the rule of Buddhist sacerdotalism. But their authority extends over several fraternities attached to the ancient national worship, and each wears the hair according to the ordinances of the sect to which they belong. There is no less variety in the costumes and liveries of the masters of ceremonies, heralds-of-arms, cooks, grooms, porters, and valets attached to the different sects of the monastery.

The grooms of Kannon-*sama* have the care of a couple of white horses, called "the horses of the goddess." These sacred horses are fed with consecrated beans, and enjoy the privilege of sleeping upright, sustained by a sort of hammock made of strong suspending bands. At morning, the priests lead them forth before the statue of Kannon, and ask her if she does not wish to go out riding. The heralds-at-arms have charge of a whole arsenal of casques and steel armour, and figure in the festivals and in the processions. The monks often give spectacles in which artists play their parts either as dancers or as comedians. On these occasions there may be seen, on the fifteenth day of the sixth month, a very curious piece—a sword-dance, or great military pantomime exclusively executed by the priests.

The triumph of Asakusa-*dera* is its *matsuri* at the end of the year. Although there is a permanent fair that is frequented by crowds every day, and is the habitual resort or playground of its great monastery, it is from the eighteenth to the last day of the twelfth month that the sacred residence of Kannon-*sama* displays all its prestige and becomes the centre of circulation, not only for several hundreds of thousands, but for three or four millions of inhabitants of the city and surrounding provinces. The entire precinct is invaded by the multitude, whose waves form regular currents that pass backward and forward under the skilful and silent direction of the police. Such perfect order in the midst of such a multitude is only possible in a city like Edo, where not only there are no vehicles, but where one word from a magistrate suffices to prohibit the use of horses and palanquins for a fortnight throughout the vast space. Thus there is no crush at any point. Cords made of straw limit the space reserved to each industry. At certain specified places there are wayside alters, and the exits and entrances are skilfully arranged. No fixed hour is named for closing, the tide of humanity rises all day, attains its height at sunset, and ebbs rapidly from midnight until dawn.

Edo Life

There was not a Japanese dwelling of the middle classes without its little garden, a sacred asylum for solitude, for the siesta, for amusing reading, for line fishing, or for long libations of tea and *sake*.

The hills on the south, west, and north of the citadel, are rich in pretty valleys and grottoes, springs and ponds, all utilized in the most ingenious manner by the small proprietors. If nature has not isolated the properties by means of hedges or natural palisades of bamboo covered with climbing plants, industry supplies the deficiency. When the garden is approached from the street, a rustic bridge is thrown across the canal before the door, and hidden with tufts of trees and thick-leaved shrubs. On crossing the threshold, the visitor might believe himself to be in a virgin forest far from all human habitations. Blocks of stone, negligently arranged as stops, help him to mount the hill; and suddenly, when he has reached the summit, a delightful spectacle lies at his feet. Below the flower-covered rocks is a gracefully formed pond, its banks adorned with lotus, iris, and waterlilies, a little wooden bridge crosses it.

The path descends through groves of tufted bamboos, azaleas, dwarf palms, and camellias, then through beautiful groups of tiny pines which hide the ivy-covered rocks, and along hillsides enamelled with flowers, amid which the lily lifts its white crown above the dwarf shrubs, which are cut into fantastic forms.

This scene, when beheld from the bottom of the valley, offers an equally harmonious combination of form and color. There is nothing to excite particular attention, but the whole landscape and all its details wrap the mind in calm, and leave it no other impression than the vague pleasure of perfect rest.

Although the Japanese delight on occasion to plunge themselves into a condition that closely approaches the physical insensibility and ideal annihilation recommended by Buddhism, they do not systematically indulge in it. The spirit of order presides over their daily conduct, and regulates their hygienic practices.

Among the latter the bath holds the first place. In addition to their morning ablutions, the Japanese, of every age and of both sexes, take a hot bath every day, at a temperature rather above that of fifty degrees centigrade. They remain from five to thirty minutes in the water, sometimes plunged up to the shoulders, sometimes only up to the waist, according as they lie down or squat. And during all the time they take the greatest care to avoid wetting the head. It not unfrequently happens that congestion of the brain, and even apoplexy, is the result of this unreasonable habit.

A custom that has become a daily need, and is practised by all classes of an enormous population, could not be in any sense private. A tacit agreement has therefore been established in Japan, which places the bath, from the point of view of public morals, in the category of indifferent actions, neither more nor less than sleeping, walking out, and drinking. As the superior classes of society have dormitories and dining rooms, so each house belonging to the nobility or the upper ranks of the citizens has one or two bathrooms reserved for domestic use. And there is no small citizen's dwelling without some little room where a bath, with its heating apparatus, may be found. When the bath is ready, the entire family profit by it in succession, first the father, then the mother, then the children and all the household servants included.

Nevertheless, the common bath is rarely used, because the expense of the fuel it would involve would be much greater than the expense of a family subscription to the public baths. Accordingly the majority of the population regularly use the latter. They are to be found in every street of a certain importance, and everywhere they are so crowded, especially during the two last hours of the day, that it has become absolutely necessary to allow the bathers to bathe in community. There are generally two reservoirs, separated by a low iron or wooden bridge, and sufficiently spacious to receive from twelve to twenty bathers at a time. The women and children collect on one side, and the men on the other. But without prejudice to the leading principle that every newcomer shall install himself where he finds a place, no matter who may be the previous occupant. The proprietor squats on a platform, from which he can observe the persons who come in, and who pay in passing. Sometimes the proprietor smokes, and sometimes he reads romances to amuse himself.

The national law that regulates the public baths extends beyond the threshold of these establishments—that is to say, if the bathers of either sex wish to take the air on the pavement outside, they are respectively regarded as partaking of the benefit of the accepted fiction. And more than that, it shelters them to their own dwelling, when it is their pleasure to proceed there with the fine lobster-color which they have brought out of the hot water intact.

However strange this custom may appear to us, no Japanese, before the arrival of the Europeans, supposed that it could have a reprehensible side. On the contrary, it was in perfect harmony with the rules of domestic life, and irreproachable from the moral point of view.

Many singularities find explanation in the fact that the Japanese have decidedly no pretension to plastic beauty. Nothing is more characteristic in this respect than the manner in which the native painters draw the heroes and heroines of their stories of love and war. In a little while, however, Japan will be under the influence of the Japanese who have visited Europe, and especially those who have made a prolonged sojourn here. If the comparison they institute between the two civilizations does not induce them to recommend the adoption of ours in its lesser details, we may be quite sure that they will reform all such national customs as have provoked the ridicule of foreigners.

Several of the great public baths of Edo have added modern therapeutic inventions, such as douches of hot and cold water, to the ordinary resources of these establishments.

The physicians of the opulent classes of society are always certain to win the good graces of their patients by recommending them to try a cure in one of the mountain districts famous for the efficacy of their waters. There are some particularly celebrated in the island of Kyushu, at the foot of the volcanoes of Aso and Taka. The thermal springs found there are, generally speaking, sulphurous and very hot. They are used for rheumatic affections and skin diseases.

It has not yet occurred to the mind of the Japanese to enhance the charms of the bathing season by the attraction of roulette and *trente et quarante*. Games of chance are disdained by everyone in good society. Cards are left to servants and coolies, and these are not permitted to play for money.

The small tradesman does not trouble himself to go to the thermal baths. When doctors do not seem to be doing him any good, he prefers to undertake a pilgrimage. He is not without his own notions about medicine. According to him the latent cause of all the disturbance of the human machine resides in the more or less ill-regulated action of the internal vapors, apparently those Molière's play *Sganarelle* describes as, "the vapors formed of the exhalations of the influences that arise from the region of the malady." The daily baths, no doubt, contribute to disengage and to dissolve them. If, however, some unexpected indisposition arises during the hours of work or of recreation, it is good to have a little medicine case at hand, and, therefore, he wears it hanging from his girdle, on the same bunch of strings with his pipe and his tobacco bag. But if the morbific gas resists the powders and the pills in his little box, he must have recourse to cautery. The former does not absolutely demand the intervention of the surgeon. Every well-arranged household has its supply of the little cones of mugwort with which *moxa* are applied, and every good housewife ought to know what are the portions of the body to burn according to the symptoms of the malady, as, for example, the shoulders in indigestion, stomach complaints, and loss of appetite, the vertebrae in attacks of pleurisy, the muscles of the thumb in a case of toothache, and so on. Such is the reputation of the moxa among the Japanese people, that it is frequently used as a preventive, and even at fixed times once or twice a year.

A sovereign remedy against cholic consists in making six or nine deep incisions, by means of fine needles of gold or silver, in the abdominal region.

As in certain countries in Europe, there exists a class of quacks who add teeth-drawing to the barber's profession, and who put on leeches and blisters, so Japan possesses a whole host of subaltern surgeons specially devoted to the practice of cautery and other empirical remedies. They are

called *tensashi*, or "men who punish," in reference to their preliminary operations. Whatever talent they may display in their various functions, they are
never allowed to massage—a kind of treatment much resorted to in Japan
in cases of nervous irritation or rheumatic affections.

The reason for this exclusion was told me by a shopkeeper, at whose
house I witnessed a spectacle that at first sight I could not understand. A
woman, lying on her left side at full length on the mats in the back shop,
was patiently bearing the weight of a big fellow, who was kneading her
shoulders with both hands. "Is that your wife? "said I to the shopkeeper. He
made an affirmative sign, and then placing his thumb and middle finger of
his left hand on his two eyelids, showed me that the operator was blind,
and went on to inform me that the laws of society among the Japanese
limited the office of masseurs to men deprived of sight. I remembered to
have met blind men in the street carefully feeling for the footway, a rough
staff in their right hand, and in the left a reed cut into a whistle, from which
they extracted a plaintive and prolonged sound at intervals. Thus they
announce to the citizens that they are passing by, in case anyone wants to
be massaged. The masseurs have the head shaven, and wear one garment,
of grey or blue material.

I was told that they form a large fraternity, which is divided into two
orders. The most ancient, that of the Tōdōza, has a religious character. It
was instituted and endowed by the son of Emperor Ninmyō, Prince
Saneyasu, who became blind by dint of weeping for the death of his empress.
All the members of this society must exercise a profession. There are some
who become musicians, special players on the *biwa*, but the greater number
practise massaging. All the money they collect from city to city is deposited
in a central treasury, from which the associates receive a fixed sum, sufficient
for their subsistence to the end of their lives. The governor of the order
resides at Kyoto. I am told that he exercises the right of life and death over
the members, subject only to the imperial supremacy.

It is not difficult for a foreigner sojourning in Japan to mix with the
people, and even to penetrate into the intimacy of the middle classes. But
I doubt whether he would ever succeed in gaining admission to family
festivals in any rank whatever of native society.

In all the countries of the far East, the marriage of a daughter is always celebrated with more or less prolonged rejoicings in the house of the husband. But, while the Chinese are proud to invite foreign guests to the wedding of their son, in order that they may make a pompous parade before them, the Japanese, on the contrary, surround the ceremonies which belong to this solemn act with the discreetest reserve. They regard it as much too serious an affair to be interfered with by the presence of any but the nearest relatives and the confidential friends of the two principals.

Most Japanese marriages are the result of family arrangement made long beforehand, under the inspiration of the practical good sense that is one of the national characteristics. The bride brings no dowry, but she is given a trousseau which many a lady of higher rank might be proud of. She is required to have an unsullied reputation, a gentle and yielding disposition, the amount of education fitted for her sex, and the acquirements of a good housekeeper. Considerations of pecuniary interest hold only a secondary place, and they generally lead rather to business combinations than to mere money bargains. Thus, when a good citizen who has no son, gives his only, or his eldest daughter in marriage, her husband receives the title of his father-in-law's adopted son, takes the name of his father-in-law, and succeeds him in the exercise of his industry, or the transaction of his commercial affairs.

Japanese weddings are preceded by a betrothal ceremony, at which the principal members of both families are present. And it not unfrequently happens that it is on this occasion the young people discover for the first time the projects their respective parents have formed for them. From that day on they are given opportunities of meeting, and of appreciating the wisdom of the choice made on their behalf. Visits, invitations, presents, preparations for their installation in their new home succeed each other so rapidly and so pleasantly, that the young people are rarely otherwise than delighted with their prospects.

The marriage generally takes place when the bride-elect has attained her sixteenth, and the bridegroom-elect his twentieth year. Early in the morning the young girl's trousseau is brought to the bridegroom's dwelling, and laid out very tastefully in the apartments in which the wedding feast is to be held. In the chief room a domestic altar is erected, adorned with flowers and laden with offerings. And in front of this altar, images of the gods and patron saints of the two families are hung. The aquariums are supplied with various plants, grouped picturesquely, and with symbolical significance. On the lacquer-work tables are placed dwarf cedars and small figures representing the first couple, accompanied by their venerable attributes, the hundred-years-old crane and tortoise. To complete the picture by a lesson in morals and patriotism, some packets of edible seaweed, of mussels and dried fish, are placed among the wedding presents, to remind the young couple of the primitive food, and the simple customs of the ancient inhabitants of Japan.

About noon a splendid procession enters the rooms thus prepared, the young bride, veiled and arrayed in white, advances, led by two female friends, and followed by a crowd of relatives, friends, and neighbors, in robes of ceremony composed of splendid scarlet brocade, gauze, and embroideries. The two friends do the honorus, distribute the guests, see to the arrangements for the repast, and flit about from one group to another. They are called the male and female butterfly. They must personify, in the cut and decoration of their crape and gauze robes, the charming couple who, in popular story, set an example of conjugal felicity. May you, too, they seem to say to the betrothed pair, taste the flowers of life, hover in aerial flight over the earth, during your terrestrial career, always joyous, always united, until your happy existence exhales in common in a final embrace.

With the exception of certain Buddhist sects, whose rites include a nuptial benediction, the priest has no place in the celebration of marriage in Japan, The decisive ceremony by which the Japanese replace our sacramental ordinance possesses an affecting symbolism. Amongst the objects displayed in the midst of the circle of the guests is a metal vase, in the form of a pitcher with two mouths. This vase is beautifully ornamented. At an appointed signal one of the bride's ladies fills it with *sake*, the other takes it by the handle, raises it to the height of the mouths of the kneeling bride and bridegroom, and makes them drink alternately, each from the pitcher mouth placed opposite to their lips, until the vase is emptied. It is thus that, husband and wife, they must drink from the cup of conjugal life, he on his side, she on hers, but they must both taste the same ambrosia, or the same gall, they must share equally the pains and sorrows as well as the joys of this new existence.

If the poetical charm of the symbolism of the natural affections sufficed to render people moral, the Japanese should be the best husbands in the world. Unhappily, the same man who has the right to kill his wife on the simplest suspicion—if, for example, he should see her in conversation with a stranger—no relation of the family—has no scruple about introducing a first concubine, and soon a second, then a third, and it may be even a fourth, under the conjugal roof.

It is said that, in order to spare the dignity of the legitimate wife, and in deference to her rank as a mother and the mistress of the house, the husband deigns to consult her on the choice of each of the pearls of beauty he thinks fit to add to the treasures of his domestic felicity. It is said that the proudest dame, the most tenacious of her rights and of her prerogatives, feels no jealousy, and sees with no displeasure an augmentation of her household that permits her to rule over a numerous suite of women, her humble servants, and little pages, slaves to the caprices of her own children. But this picture is not true to life.

There is, no doubt, a class in Japanese society in which the marriage tie is much relaxed, that of the *daimyō*, formerly condemned by the inhuman policy of the *shōgun* to leave their wives and children as hostages at Edo, during the prolonged absences rendered imperative by their feudal position and its administrative duties. But the licentious habits of the nobility never propagate themselves among the middle classes with impunity. When the mother of the family forces herself to suffer humiliation in silence, from then on peace and domestic happiness are at an end. When the relaxation of the ties of esteem and mutual confidence leads to a breach of the community of interests, disorder creeps into household affairs, the husband neglects the exercise of his profession, and endeavours to blind himself to his true moral condition, by an ever increasing consumption of *sake*. Finally, poverty, sickness, and frequently even some violent catastrophe, bring about the dissolution or the ruin of the household, which had been founded under such fair auspices.

The middle classes, and the masses in general, are saved by their narrow means from the scourge I have just indicated. The great majority of households, those of shopkeepers, artizans, workmen, and cultivators, require the common toil of both father and mother for their maintenance,

Bakumatsu Japan

the constant combination of their efforts, not to secure ease, but merely to supply the commonest necessaries of life.

The introduction of one single vice into such a state of things would bring about its immediate ruin. Many a young couple have to struggle bravely for years, in order to defray the expenses of their marriage. Others have had sufficient courage and good sense to resist the temptation of the national custom. The proceedings in the latter instances testify to the national talent for acting. An honest couple have a marriageable daughter, and the latter is acquainted with a fine young fellow, who would be a capital match, if only he possessed the necessary means of making his lady-love and her parents the indispensable wedding presents, and of keeping open house for a week. One fine evening, the father and mother, returning from the bath, find the house empty—the daughter is gone. They make inquiries in the neighborhood, but no one has seen her. The neighbors hasten to offer their services in seeking her, together with her distracted parents. They accept the offer, and head a solemn procession, which goes from street to street, to the lover's door. In vain does the lover, hidden behind his panels, turn a deaf ear. At length he is obliged to yield to the importunities of the besieging crowd. He opens the door, and the young girl, drowned in tears, throws herself at the feet of her parents, who threaten to curse her. Then comes the intervention of charitable friends, deeply moved by this spectacle, the softening of the mother, the proud and inexorable attitude of the father, the combined eloquence of the multitude, employed to soften his heart, the lover's endless protestations of his resolution to become the best of sons-in-law. At length the father yields, his resistance is overcome, he raises his kneeling daughter, pardons her lover, and calls him his son-in-law. Then, almost as if by enchantment, cups of *sake* circulate through the assembly, everybody sits down on the mats, the two culprits are placed in the centre of the circle, large bowls of *sake* are handed to them. And when they are emptied, the marriage is recognized, and declared to be validly contracted in the presence of a sufficient number of witnesses, and it is registered next day by the proper officer, without any difficulty.

The fashion of wedding trips is unknown in Japan. Far from leaving the young people to enjoy their happiness in peace, their friends resort to every sort of pretext for overwhelming them with invitations and visits, which are always accompanied by prolonged bouts of eating and drinking.

As soon as the young wife has the hope of becoming a mother, all her relatives, near and distant, assemble at her house, and the announcement of the good news is welcomed by a concert of coarse congratulations, indiscreet questions, and hygienic confidences absolutely untranslatable. The young wife is, from this moment, placed under the direction of an experienced matron, called the *oba-san*, whose sole real service consists in making herself an indispensable fixture in the house for the rest of her days. At the third month a fresh solemnity takes place, no less difficult to describe than the first. On this occasion the *oba-san* unfolds, exhibits to the company, and finally invests her charge with the girdle of red cords, which is only to be laid aside on the completion of the sixth month. When the time of delivery approaches, the poor patient is surrounded by a crowd of friends, relations, and neighbors, and is obliged to submit with humble resignation to the suffering imposed by the orders of the *oba-san*, and the contradictory advice of her innumerable counsellors. The birth of the child does but redouble their officiousness. An incomprehensible prejudice deprives the young mother of the necessary sleep her whole being craves, and she is not allowed a moment's repose until her child, having been washed and dressed, is placed in her arms.

Here commences the second phase of her conjugal career. For two years at least she will nurse the child, and according to the rules of politeness that regulate the visits of Japanese ladies, she must extend her lacteal gifts to the children of her friends. Another demonstration of courtesy is made by the young girls of the neighborhood. They dispute for the privilege of carrying the new-born infant out for its air and exercise, not only as an act of neighborly kindness, but in order that they may, quite seriously, serve an apprenticeship to the main duties of their future vocation.

On the thirtieth day after his birth, the new citizen of Japan receives his first name. He will take a second on attaining his majority, a third at his marriage, a fourth when he shall be appointed to any public function, a fifth when he shall ascend in rank or in dignity, and so on until the last, the name that shall be given him after his death, and inscribed on his tomb, that by which his memory shall be held sacred from generation to generation.

The ceremony, which corresponds to baptism among us, is a simple presentation of the newly-born child in the temple of his parents' gods. Except in certain sects, it is not accompanied by sprinkling with water, or any of the formalities of purification. The father hands a memorandum containing three names, to the officiating monk, who copies them on three separate sheets of paper, which he mixes together and shakes up at random, pronouncing a sacramental invocation in a loud voice. Then he throws them into the air, and the first which, in falling, touches the floor of the holy place, indicates the name most agreeable to the presiding divinity. The monk immediately inscribes it on a sheet of blessed paper, and gives it as a talisman to the child's father. Then, the religious act being complete, it remains only to celebrate the event by visits and banquets proportionate to the social condition of the infant hero of the festival, who receives a number of presents on this occasion, among which two fans, in the case of a male, and a pot of pomade in that of a female child. The fans are precursors of swords, and the pomaded is the presage of feminine charms. In both cases, a packet of flax thread is added, signifying good wishes for a long life.

The baptism of a child is always an occasion for generosity on the part of the parent towards the priests of their religion. It is understood that the priests shall not fail to inscribe the child's name on the list of their pupils, and shall follow all the phases of his life with solicitude. The registers in the monasteries are said to be most accurately kept, they must always be at the disposal of the police authorities.

At three years old, the boy begins to wear a sword belt, and at seven, if he is a *samurai*, the two swords, which form the insignia of his rank. These weapons are, of course, provisional, and adapted to his size. At fifteen, he exchanges them for the proven swords confided to him, as a glorious trust, by his family, during his lifetime.

In the middle class, the chivalrous ceremonies have no place, but the three beforementioned dates, and chiefly the last, are kept with rejoicings that yield in importance, only to marriage festivities. On the day that completes the boy's fifteenth year, he attains his majority, adopts the headdress of grown men, and takes a part in the business of the paternal house. The day before he is addressed as a child, all of a sudden everything around him is changed, the ceremonious forms of national civility increase his importance in his own eyes, and he hastens, on his side, to respond to the congratulations he receives, so as to prove that while he is proud of his new position, he is also awake to its responsibility. This noble testimony does not, indeed, limit itself to vain declarations. Among the most interesting traits of Japanese society are the zeal, perseverance, and seriousness with which young people of fifteen forsake the pleasures of childhood, and enter the severe school of practical life, preparing themselves to make their way honorably in the world.

Apprenticeship to any manual profession is equivalent to ten years' service. During this time the master feeds, clothes, and lodges the apprentice, but he never gives him any salary, until quite near the end of the term, when the apprentice having become a workman, receives sufficient pocket money to buy tobacco. Professional instruction does not suffer from this state of things. The master is interested in teaching his apprentice as thoroughly as possible, because it is he who presents the workman, in his turn aspiring to the rank of master, to the tribe or trade. This rank cannot be attained under the age of twenty-five years. As soon as the workman has reached that time of life, his master gives him his liberty, and presents him with the tools necessary for the setting up of a modest workshop. Then comes marriage to consecrate the new establishment.

It frequently happens that the workman marries before he is set up in a workshop of his own. But this takes place only when his parents' circumstances admit of his bringing his wife to live under their roof until he can make a home for her.

In all Japanese families death gives rise to a series of domestic solemnities, more or less sumptuous, according to the rank of the deceased, but in every case in a proportion very expensive to his nearest relatives. They have to bear the cost of the religious ceremonies, which are in the province of the monks. They have to pay for the last sacraments, the watching and the praying, which is kept up without intermission in the house of the deceased until the funeral, the service that precedes the departure of the funeral procession, the funeral mass celebrated in the temple, and all the requisites for the burial or the burning of the corpse, such as the coffin, draperies, torches, flowers, combustibles, urn, tomb, collections and offerings given to the monks. Then comes the turn of the coolies who have washed the body, of those who have carried the coffin, and the convent servants whose duties lie within the enclosure of the cemetery. But this is not all, a pious custom ordains that all persons of a certain station shall install a servant at the house door charged with the distribution of alms, in small coins, to all the poor, indiscriminately, who come to seek them. On the return of the funeral procession, all the party are expected to take leave of the head of the afflicted family, who testifies his gratitude by giving them a handsome repast.

It is not in these harassing expenses only that we must seek for the source of the hardly disguised impatience with which the Japanese discharge the last offices towards their neighbors. The truth is, that though they are hardened to the sight of blood, and to scenes of homicide, they cannot overcome, even in the case of members of their own family, the instinctive repugnance, the profound horror the presence or even the vicinity of a corpse causes them, when the death has been a natural one.

There are noble exceptions. Among the Japanese women, we find wives and mothers, who, overcoming every superstitious fear, know how to prove that love is stronger than death, while the men of the household consider themselves acquitted of their task when they have sent for the monks to recite prayers, and for a barber and his coolie assistants, who lay out the corpse, and retire to smoke and drink at the greatest possible distance from the chamber of death, the mother of the family remains to the last beside the corpse of the husband or the son. During the first hours of mourning, it is she who receives the condolences of the friends and neighbors. Humbly prostrated on the reversed mat, at the foot of a screen, also reversed, which hides the corpse from view, she mingles her sobs with the sighs and consoling words of her visitors. But as soon as the undertakers (as we should call them), arrive, she rises and assists in all the preparations they have to make. The head of the deceased must be completely shaven, and the body carefully washed, which is done by plentiful douches of tepid water, showered into the bathroom in which it is placed sitting on a turned up tub. When the coolies have dried the corpse, they lift it up respectfully, in order to place it in the coffin. The operation is not always an easy one. The rich Japanese who favor inhumation, like to rest in the earth, doubled up into enormous jars, which are masterpieces of native pottery. It requires a certain amount of energy and very strong wrists to squeeze a corpse that is at all broad-shouldered into the narrow neck of one of these jars.

The lower middle class and common people use, for coffins, simply barrels made of fir planks, with bands of bamboo bark. Whether the corpse is going to be buried or burned, it is squeezed into the same narrow compass. The head is bent, the legs are doubled up under the body, and the arms are crossed on the breast. It is not accidentally that the Japanese bury their dead in the attitude in which a child rests in the mother's womb. The practice enforces the dogma of a future life under an eloquent symbolism, of which the concluding action of the final parting is a most significant feature. At the moment when the coolies are about to place the cover on the jar, or the lid on the barrel, the mourning woman who has previously assisted in all the melancholy preliminaries, bends for the last time over the corpse, and places between its hands a viaticum, no doubt the strangest, but also the most remarkable in all the mythologies of antiquity. It is a little sheet of paper, folded in four, containing a small shred of the umbilical cord which united the dead person with his mother at the moment of his birth. When maternal love, or that of his successor has confided this strange emblem of a future birth to the mysteries of the tomb, and made, under this curious form, its humble protest against the seeming triumph of death, the coffin is closed. And the most important of the national funeral ceremonies, the domestic solemnity is accomplished.

The rest consists merely of superstitious practices, vain pomp, and pure formalities, in which exorcism alternates with the glorification of family pride. It does not suffice that the *mikoshi* should protect the coffin, at its exit from the house of death, it passes under an arch of blessed bamboo, which prevents evil influences from The monks, carrying their rosaries, open the procession. The nearest relatives are dressed in white, or wear common straw hats, which they do not remove until after the completion of the ceremonies of purification. An inscription, carried before the *mikoshi*, proclaims the name which the deceased is to receive in his epitaph. The horses of a military chief figure in his funeral procession, caparisoned in white, and led by grooms in mourning. His swords, his armorial bearings, his banner, various precious things that recall the rank that he held in the world, are exhibited among the groups of his relations and followers.

The funeral procession of the poor man consists of a small number of friends and neighbors, who hurry, at sunset, to the sombre valley where the vulgar rite of incineration takes place under the auspices of some monk of low station, sent from a neighboring convent.

The *eta*, who are the pariahs of Japanese society, and deprived of the aids of religion, disdain every kind of ceremony. They simply lay the corpses of their brethren in abjectness on rude stretchers, and carry them away to a deserted place. There, they pile up a heap of dead wood on which they stretch the bodies, covered with straw mats, and kindle with their own hands the fire that is to restore these miserable remains of humanity to the elements.

There is a class still lower than that of the *eta*, properly so called, that is to say the artisans who practise unclean arts, such as skinners, tanners, leather dressers. And one lower still, public executioners, purveyors of vice, lepers, cripples, registered beggars. Then comes a final category of individuals held in the extreme degree of legal infamy, it is the class of Christans, the tolerated descendants of such of the native Christian families as were not entirely destroyed in the great persecution of the 17th century. Their condition is worse than that of the *eta*, who live among themselves in freedom, outside the city boundaries, so utterly ignored by the law, that the space of ground occupied by their camp of thatched huts does not count in the measurement plans. The Christans, on the contrary, are assigned a miserable crowded quarter in the city, like the ghetto of the Jews in the Middle Ages, which is virtually a prison. The police keep watch over them until they have drawn their last breath, and it is their business to remove the corpses, and dispose of them somehow—no one knows where or how. But so that the name of the crucified one shall not be pronounced over their ashes.

Respect for the dead, and tomb-worship, which is one of the seemingly estimable features of the Buddhist religion, does not exist, properly speaking, except among the privileged classes, and in proportion to the profit the monks extract from it. The method of inhumation, the form of the coffin, and especially the practice of incineration, introduced, in the year 700, by the priest Dōshō, have enabled the monks to make an immense trade out of the lots of ground of which they dispose. A small enclosure is sufficient for a whole family through a great number of generations. The commemorative table, which stands over the spot in which the cinerary urn has been buried, occupies no greater space than the urn itself. The badly-kept condition of the burial-places of the common people contrasts strongly with the orderliness of the fine terraces and great funereal monuments in their neighborhood. Both are entrusted to the care of the same monastery. But it is the same with tombs as with indulgences, the monks have made each a question of tariff.

Street Life

Public performers form a corporation independent of the fraternity of comedians. They are, properly speaking, jugglers, equilibrists, and acrobats, of whom it is easy to form an idea, since several of them have been for years exhibiting in Europe. Another corporation, infinitely more interesting, is that of the conjuring jugglers, the most skilful among whom perform principally at the fair of Yamashita, and in all the dependencies of the Kannon temple at Asakusa. They also make provincial tours, although we have not heard of their having quitted Japan. But we may leave them aside, and even their superiors, and pass on to the monasteries of the Kannon temple in the district of Asakusa-Imato, which combine within their vast space all the seductions and all the jugglers, every industry and every artifice, by which it is possible to contribute to human superstitions and passions.

The great Sumida River that divides Edo into two distinct cities, encloses in one vast circuit the districts to the north of the citadel. Two portions of the town of Edo are known by the name of Asakusa Okuramaya, the region of teahouses, and Asakusa Imato the region of monasteries. The two Asakusas are specially consecrated to the pleasures of the inhabitants of the capital. In those pleasures centers the industry of the district, and it excludes no class of society. It accommodates itself, on the contrary, to all tastes, responds to all caprices, and satisfies all exigencies.

Hundreds of temples rival the teahouses, the circuses compete with the theaters, the fairs with the groves, the lakes, and the canals—those refuges of tranquil joy, while towards the north, in the solitude of the rice fields of Asakusa Imato, the great square, which we may almost call the city of Shin-Yoshiwara, harbours, with the full sanction of the government, countless dens of vice and debauchery.

The northern road beyond Sumida Kawabata is divided into two branches, one branch leads directly to the great temple of Asakusa, the other borders the river as far as the quarter of the theaters. From there it enters the rice fields and takes the direction of Senjōbashi. On the right and left of the high road, and all along the avenues of Asakusa-*dera*, on the bank of the Sumida-*gawa*, and in the side streets which diverge from the high road, there are temples, teahouses, public gardens, eating houses, oratories, shops, and wayside alters, booths in which consecrated rosaries and profane curiosities are exhibited—in a word, everything that the most ingenious speculation can offer to the travellers, the pilgrims, the frequenters of theaters, and the idlers of all ages, who are coming and going by thousands, by night as well as by day, through these distant quarters of the capital.

There are almost within the same district, and generally throughout the meridional zone of the triangle formed by the Sumida-*gawa* two kinds of tea houses. They only prosper at a certain distance from the great arteries of circulation, because their speciality consists in keeping themselves apart from the floating population, while permitting their frequenters to mingle for a few minutes, when they please, with the movements of the crowd. The first are the aristocratic teahouses. They can hardly be distinguished externally from those of the middle classes. Their entire superiority consists in the arrangement of the halls and of the furniture, of the garden, and above all in the ceremony of the entertainments.

When the haughty *samurai* enters one of these establishments, the mistress of the house, and the young waitresses who accompany her, prostrate themselves at his feet. The youngest of the girls rises, and begs the favor of carrying the sword of the noble person, who presents it to her. She hastens to unfold a silken handkerchief, with which she covers her right hand, in order to take hold of the sword by the end of the scabbard, and she holds it in front of her breast until the *samurai* has gone into the vestiary, when she places it on a lacquered rack. The gentleman then proceeds, with the aid of his female suite, to make the most luxurious and minute nocturnal toilet. The one lock of hair that constitutes his headdress is twisted by means of a knot of crape into a sort of nightcap. On his neck and shoulders is laid a thick silken handkerchief, which serves him for a shawl. His cloak is replaced by a sumptuous dressing gown, fastened by silken cords most gracefully disposed, a pair of white socks, which serve as slippers, completes his costume, and after having washed his hands and face in perfumed water, he majestically takes his way to the salon, where a collation is prepared. It is a rule for houses of this rank to maintain a very numerous staff, so that it would be considered beneath their dignity to have recourse to the services of professional singers, guitar players, and dancers. It is only in the inferior restaurants and other public places that such persons may be engaged either by the night or by the hour.

These women, on their side, never set their feet in such establishments, unless they are expressly sent for. In this respect, as well as by the correctness of their behavior, they are distinguished from the street musicians and the dancers at fairs. The law does not permit them to come into private houses, they can only be asked for in places subject to police regulation. Theatres are comprised in this category, they appear there at the request of the performers in the plays in order to figure in the ballet.

The other teahouses I indicated are also reckoned highly distinguished. They are patronized by retired functionaries, officers without ambition, or merchants who have made their fortunes—peaceful people and very exclusive, who during the day require nothing but shade, freshness, retirement, and silence, and in the evening hours the quiet chat on the verandah in front of the groves and the garden tank. Sometimes the hostess or one of her young attendants is invited to take part in the conversation. Women of this class are renowned for their wit and freedom of speech. They conduct themselves with graceful modesty towards men in good society, but they encounter with perfect ease the barrack talk of the *yakunin*. This is not a symptom of effrontery on their part; it is merely the effect of national education, which permits both sexes indifferently to speak of everything without the slightest periphrasis, or any respect for persons, even for children.

This excessive liberty of speech is common to the Japanese of every rank, but it must not be confused with laxity in morals, which, even among unmarried women, is much less general than we might be tempted to suppose. Women of the class to which I am alluding are not supposed to advertise themselves so shamelessly in Japan as they are in Europe, it is only by a certain exceptional headdress and luxurious costume that the livery of vice can be recognized. Outside the enclosure of Shin-Yoshiwara, and especially in the northern quarters, it may be perceived under various forms, but none of them are indecent. Among the crowd of boats on the Sumida-*gawa* we may perhaps notice an elegant gondola, in which a young girl, negligently leaning against the roof of the cabin, attracts attention by her tasteful attire. Her long robe, in particular, will be distinguished, by some strange embroidery which facilitates the recognition of her person. For example, it may be a double wreath of bats, one black and the other white. Suddenly the girl will draw out of her girdle a roll of tissue paper, which forms the Japanese handkerchief, and slinking it with the right hand, will give a discreet signal, which no doubt has been understood, for she immediately changes the course of the gondola, which is speedily propelled towards the shore in the direction of the teahouse, the number on whose lantern corresponds with that on the prow of her boat.

Again, on the footpaths of the northern road, another girl, not less strangely attired, seems to have set herself the task of guiding benighted travellers, who have not yet made choice of a place of abode, to a neighboring hotel, by the seductive play of her rich fan. Two hundred thousand travellers on average are lodged every night in this city of vice and its suburbs. They are of all orders, and of all conditions. But no class escapes the vigilance of the female hotel keepers. Those who are posted in the proximity of the theaters belong to establishments of a very inferior rank, thus their toilet displays neither silk nor velvet—the only thing they can allow themselves is a little prodigality in the material of their girdle and in the sleeves of their *kimono*. They add a few mock tortoiseshell pins to their headdress, and they carry a little paper lantern painted in the most brilliant colors. All who succeed to this third category hide themselves from the light. Sometimes under the spacious roof of a teahouse we may see the servants watching from an angle of the gallery, and clapping their hands to attract the attention of the passers-by.

Other servants, of a still lower condition, the poor little slaves of the tavern keepers, wander in the darkness of the foetid alleys. But where must we look for the lowest degree of abject misery? Are we to find its type in the poor girl who lingers about the bridges shuddering with cold, and hardly decently covered by her single garment of thin cotton? Or must we look for her in the depths of the abyss of Shin-Yoshiwara? The police of Edo can tell us this with hideous precision, for there it levies its infamous tribute, and enforces the code of female slavery, not only for that portion of the city which knows no other rule, but in all the hotels and among all the lodging house keepers, whose privilege is sanctioned alike by law and custom.

Not one of these unfortunates is permitted to free herself from her owners, neither is there one who escapes the vigilance of the authorities, which does not extend beyond purely police and fiscal action. Nothing whatever is done in the interest of the public health. All attempts in that direction made by Europeans, in the ports open to them, are frustrated by the insurmountable repugnance of the natives. From year to year this horrible evil extends in every grade of society, and assumes more and more strongly the characteristics of a national scourge, and an immense public calamity.

We made frequent morning excursions to the Fukagawa quarter, which forms the southern suburb of Honjo. On reaching the shore we could see the quays of Takanawa, Hamagoten, Teppōzu, and the block of the city over which the enormous roof of the temple of Monzeki towers. We have frequently ascended the coast of the Ishikawa Island at the mouth of the Sumida River, and, turning to the left, disembarked behind the fortifications and the government docks on the southern extremity of Honjo.

The streets in the vicinity of the harbour are the centre of innumerable industries, whose raw materials are furnished by the ocean. There we saw vast drying houses for the fish, molluscs, and seaweed destined for exportation, and also the great stages on which the preparations of the *aburagami*, or oil paper material used by the Japanese instead of our waterproof materials, are stretched.

The native artizans excel in the fabrication and imitation of the edible birds' nests of Java. They produce these forgeries by means of a glutinous exudation of certain marine herbs, and they are then exported to China, with every trick in their packing and labelling that can possibly deceive the experts of China. And I am by no means sure that Europe has not also been extensively taken in.

Fish sausages are extensively made in this quarter. They are of various kinds, each having a special color. A great whitewashed oven is set up in the centre of a spacious kitchen, it contains bowls of iron, and a jar in which a certain class of fish is cooking. Others are chopped up very small. As soon as they are sufficiently dried and reduced to a powder in mortars of hard wood, they are sorted, seasoned, and rolled into paste, pressed, and tied up in their envelopes, of which each receives its dip of color. They are then packed in bales. Half a dozen persons generally work together on all these operations, which are performed to a monotonous song. The knives and the pestles are used in time to the rhyme. But when any noise comes from the street the men throw them down and go out and swell the gaping crowd.

Perhaps nothing more serious is going on than the lion dance. How often everyone there has seen it! And nevertheless the discordant appeal of the fife and the tambourine announcing its approach is never resisted.

Four actors come out of a neighboring street, three form the orchestra, and the fourth gives the representation. He is wrapped in a very large striped cloak surmounted by an enormous lion's head. The monster can make himself longer or shorter at will, and suddenly raise himself up two yards above the people who are with him. The children utter cries of mingled admiration and fear. Some, bolder than the rest, venture to lift up the skirts of his cloak, and even to pinch the legs of the mysterious tumbler. He sometimes frightens them, by turning his head towards them, opening his mouth, and shaking the thick mane of scraps of white paper surrounding his scarlet face. Then he begins to dance to the sound of the instruments of his companions. He carries his tambourine himself, but as soon as he leaves off dancing he sets it down, and, suddenly stooping, transforms himself into a quadruped, executes some grotesque gambols, and finishes by stripping off his accoutrements. Then the monster vanishes, but the juggler remains. He seizes a drumstick and balances it on the thumb of the left hand. He puts a second stick on the end of the first, and a third crosswise above the other two. Finally, he throws them into the air, catches them in his hands, and spins them about more and more rapidly and uninterruptedly, adding one, two, or three balls coming from no one knows where.

The admiration of the spectators is at its height. One of the musicians passes round a plate—that is to say, a fan. The performance is over, and the juggler lights his pipe from that of some benevolent neighbor. It is not uncommon to see him negligently putting on his costume again, and sitting calmly smoking, his head covered down to his nose with the enormous and grotesque mask of the monster. The latter is the most picturesque part of the spectacle.

By degrees, as we penetrate into the streets and populous places of the suburb, we discover a whole world of small trades and small pleasures. Here and there we see the humble dwellings of various classes of wandering workmen who start for the city before the sun rises, and who will only return late at night. These are cobblers, who go about mending wooden sandals, tinkers, coopers, traffickers in broken porcelain, vendors of old clothes and remnants of material for girdles and women's *kimono*. All these people are trained to the exercise of great patience, and also to the calculation of fractions of fractions. It is a very curious sight to watch them counting on their frames of beads strung on wires.

We must not forget the rag-picker of Edo, who unconsciously contributed for many years to the maintenance of the paper factories in England. In the morning and the evening he goes ferreting about in the public places, and in the populous streets of Honjo and the merchant city, laden, not with a hod, but with a sort of paper basket he carries in his left hand. In his right hand is a pair of long canes, by means of which he picks up everything that appears worth the trouble, and throws it into the basket.

The professional tramps pay no attention to the curiosities they meet in their path. Nevertheless, at Edo I have seen them exchange some amicable phrases, accompanied by two or three puffs of tobacco, with their natural friends the tumblers, with whom the good city abounds. These performers go about with a kind of Punch and Judy Show, but it is really a doll with joints, arrayed in the costume of the sect of jumping priests. They exhibit, on a table, a model of the temple of Amida. A white mouse runs up the steps, rings a bell at the door, and performs its devotions at the altar. A third exhibitor goes about with birds trained to fire a bow, to pick rice, to draw water out of a well. And to pull a little car laden with balls of cotton. A street juggler balances himself on two high planks, and turns somersaults, or spins over his head three or four porcelain jugs or cups, he breaks an egg, and pulls twenty yards of string out of it. He crumples a bit of paper in his hand, and immediately a cloud of artificial flies fills the air.

The greater number of these schemers speculate less on the receipts of their representation than on the sale of certain small wares the city shopkeepers let them sell on commission. Marionettes and mice exhibitors bring crowds of children round the box they use as a stage, and these children know well that the box is full of sweetmeats. The mender of fans has a store of new ones. Other street actors bring specimens of the industry of the suburbs into the aristocratic quarters, and get a small commission on all orders they succeed in obtaining.

They also sell packets of the hard wood or bamboo canes they use for forks, also toothpicks of scented and savory wood, toothbrushes made of white wood, with one of the ends beaten out into a little fringe.

The Japanese have a peculiar tooth powder, one of its ingredients is, I am told, ivory dust. It is sold in small boxes, with variously colored and decorated lids, which vary according to the quality of the merchandise. The powder with which married women dye their teeth black is sold in metal caskets.

Workmen of the most humble appearance, cabinet makers, joiners, turners, and wood carvers, fabricate a multitude of pretty things, in elm-wood bark, bamboo, bone, ivory, deerhorn, yellow amber, seashells, tortoiseshell, and cocoanut.

The Chinese workmen who carve ivory excel in the execution of masterpieces of patience, such as little empty balls, three or four in number, which turn one within the other. The Japanese artists do not build their fame on conquering difficulties, a more noble ambition animates them. They aim above all at the perfection of the imitation of nature, and when they yield to the caprice of their imagination, it usually takes a humorous direction, full of genuine mirth, and not the taste for burlesque and eccentricity that characterizes the Chinese workman. The most exquisite things among the small figures in ivory to be found in Edo are incontestably those representing animals, and more particularly the tiger, the ox, the bear, the monkey, and the mouse. These little art objects, which for us are only curious, are an integral part of the outfit of the native smokers of both sexes. In order to carry their pipe in its case and their tobacco box, they fasten them to the end of a silken cord, whose either extremity is ornamented with one or two of these dainty little trifles, which keep down the cord and prevent it slipping when it has been passed through the girdle. They do the same with their medicine box.

I remarked at Fukagawa a very curious assemblage of large and small trades, the greater part very vulgar, but all, without exception, worthy of observation. The weavers' trade is not only applied to silk and cotton, but to canvas, which the Japanese painters use very largely. And to flax cloth, which cannot be of an inferior quality in a country like Japan, where the most precious of our European textiles grows to two yards in height.

The workshops of the hosiers, mat-borderers, binders, and box makers present a picturesque assemblage of workpeople of all ages and of both sexes. The coopers work in spacious enclosures behind bamboo palings. The shops of the box makers contain an immense collection of coffers and caskets in wood of every kind, among which the camphor wood of Kyushu, which never loses its aromatic perfume, is particularly remarkable. An assortment of these boxes means half a dozen, which can be placed one within the other so as to be packed in a single parcel. There is also an immense quantity of very strong boxes in lacquered paper, an infinite variety of household utensils, and small articles of furniture, some lacquered, such as rice bowls, others in white wood or in bamboo.

The extreme scarcity of mechanical appliances at the disposal of the Japanese artizans strikes the European visitor forcibly. Near the shops or warehouses of which I am speaking were four or five booths, which were assigned to as many different trades. I am convinced that all the tools of the five workshops put together were not worth five pounds.

In the first booth a man was making dolls of *papier mâché*, which are especial favorites in Japanese houses. They consist of the head and the face only, wrapped in a scarlet mantle. And it is said that in this form they perpetuate from generation to generation the memory of a high priest of Buddha who had used up his legs completely in the practice of his devotions. These dolls can be turned inside out, and are of all dimensions.

Further on were two workmen, each using a little hammer and chisel in carving metal pipes, and a third was preparing wooden stems, here a lounger was holding wood before the flames of a fire of shavings in order to give it the necessary bend. Meanwhile his companion was putting together with a little cement and string the tufts of silk, horse hair or paper, which are hoisted at the ends of long pikes in order to indicate the rank or functions of a civil or military chief. In a neighboring workshop an old man was adjusting the hoops and hooks of a number of paper lanterns with a pair of pincers.

At the entrance of a side street we see half a dozen workmen making wooden sandals. Here the work is divided, everyone has his speciality. One cuts a piece of wood into equal lengths with a saw, and then splits them into soles or cross planks. A third rounds the edges of the heavy sandals, and a fourth makes holes in them, through which the straw cords are passed. Other workmen are employed in finishing sandals of a more luxurious kind, and packing them by dozens of pairs into the bales that are to be carried to the retail warehouse.

I had yet to see the most peculiar of the shops in this quarter, that of the clockmaker. He was making small dials and clocks, rivalling the so-called cuckoos of the black forest, but with this difference, that they are on the system of moveable hours, which increase or decrease according to the seasons. The artist, squatting before a little anvil fixed in the ground, is busy with the mechanism of his chronometer, with the exception of the gong that strikes the hours. His tools, scattered round him on mats, consist of a hammer, two or three files, a couple of pincers, and some gimlets. With the exterior of the small dials, which are portable instruments of the form and size of a big chestnut, he has nothing to do, the cases are made by the copper workers.

Shin-Yoshiwara

Where goes that poorly-dressed woman, holding by the hand a young girl seven years of age, decked out in her best clothes? After having laid her offering before the altar of Kannon, she slowly traverses the road across the rice fields, which turns to the east, to the Shin-Yoshiwara. After an hour's walking, she reaches the wall of the city of vice, accessible only on one side—that of the north. She has met no woman on her way. The elegant palanquins of the ladies, whose coolies are carrying them in that direction, are closely shut. Individuals of every rank meet in the city, but without saluting each other, without exchanging the smallest politeness. Those who belong to the class of *samurai* hide themselves in a complete disguise.

The houses on both sides of the public way appear to be dependencies of the privileged quarter. The most miserable are tenanted by an immense population of coolies and palanquin bearers, brick-a-brack sellers, and mat plaiters. The larger houses contain bathing establishments, provision sheds, stores of bad books, restaurants, lottery offices, and taverns, in which the apparent toleration of the police adroitly conceals the control which is in reality exercised over the dangerous classes of the capital. A bridge crosses the canal through the rice fields. Nothing which takes place in this neighborhood escapes the notice of a double post of *yakunin* installed before the gates in two guard rooms opposite one another. The gatekeeper on duty conducts the poor traveller with her child into the presence of his chief.

After a few minutes, the mother and the daughter come out of the guard room, accompanied by a police agent, who leads them to one of the chief buildings in the street. This is the residence of the functionary known as

110

the chief of the great Gankirō brothel. The mother returns alone, carrying in the sleeve of her *kimono* a sum of money, amounting to about the value of 100 francs (£4 sterling). The bargain she has made is duly signed and sealed. She has sold her child, body and soul, for a term of seventeen years.

The countries of the far East suffering from an excess of population are those in which the inhuman, fundamentally antisocial, unnatural character of Buddhist paganism is revealed in all its horrors. Its every form of pagan worship finds an accomplice in the measures the governments of China and Japan have taken to preserve their cities from the invasion of Christian civilization. The opposition put in the way of native intercourse with foreigners, the absolute prohibition imposed on their desire to leave their native country, have been the true causes of the overcrowding of maritime cities. In order to remedy this evil, Buddhism, which is its real origin, palliates and absolves everything resorted to by perversity, in order to stop the progress of population. Thus Buddhism tolerates polygamy and infanticide in China, concubinage in Japan. In both countries it tolerates prostitution organized under every form, brought within the reach of all classes of society, and fed without scruple by all the resources of speculation. This includes the traffic in children under age, or, indeed, in children of every age, because here majority is only an illusory right when brought into conflict with the will of parents.

In the greater number of cases these poor creatures are the victims of the ill-conduct of the father, who has fallen into dissolute habits, and who, in order that he may be perfectly without restraint, has turned his wife and children out of their home. Japanese wives have no security against a rupture of the conjugal bond, which may be broken by the husband with no greater formality than the procuring of a letter of divorce. The forsaken wife will never have an opportunity of contracting a second marriage. Society condemns her. If she has no relations who will receive her, she is left to utter solitude, and her only prospect is poverty. Under such conditions, to give up a child under age to the Gankirō[1] is to save her from destitution, and to

---

1 The Gankirō was the "tea house" run by Satō Sakichi, alias Iwatsukiya Sakichi, the headman of the Shin-Yoshiwara licensed quarters. The name Gankirō is said to have derived from the Chinese reading of the first two characters (Iwatsuki) of Sakichi's alias, which would read "*ganki*," though it was written with different characters. Among the quarter's many brothels, the Gankirō was one of the most extravagant, so much so that daytime visitors could admire it's splendor against an admission fee.

defer, at least for a time, her own penury. If the girl is grown up, the bargain is still more advantageous, because the mother will derive from it an annual income of 100 or 200 francs (£4 or £8 sterling) during four or five years.

But what becomes of the girl when the contract has expired? She does not retain a farthing of the money her wretched profession has brought her. She has generally been allowed to get into debt, for dresses and for food, to the chief of the Gankirō. In order to discharge her obligations she is obliged to form a new engagement, so that she generally ends her life as a servant, or an overlooker, or a housekeeper, in the house where her career began. If it sometimes happen that a man forms an attachment to a courtesan, purchases her, and even marries her—that is a very exceptional case, and might happen in any country, but which we cannot regard as general in Japan.

Within the quadrangular enclosure of Shin-Yoshiwara nine distinct quarters exist, each in the form of a parallelogram stretching from east to west. On the left of the great gate there are five, on the right there are four. The former are separated from the latter by a long and spacious avenue of trees, which forms a beautiful promenade. At one end is a watchtower. Where the three angles of the city meet is a shrine, built out from the wall of the enclosure. A wide cross avenue in the centre of the quarter on the right also looks like a public promenade. But it is reserved for the inhabitants and visitors of the first-class houses by which it is surrounded. There, either by day or by night, according to the seasons, the feminine notabilities of the Gankirō are to be found walking up and down, all dressed in the invariable *kimono*, loaded with embroidery, and in a marvellous head attire of tortoiseshell combs and pins. Each of these women is accompanied by two or three pupils attached to her personal service.

These young followers wear the colors of their mistress, and an elegant headdress of artificial flowers.

The great ladies of Shin-Yoshiwara have their apartments and their reception rooms furnished with extreme elegance. Some of them are "under the protection" of young men of high family, who pay a stated sum to the chief of the Gankirō. The secrecy of such relations, more easily hidden than others from parental vigilance, gives them a peculiarly dangerous character. The women take advantage of this secrecy to gratify to the full extent their taste for luxury and ornament. More than one patrimony is swallowed up in the satisfaction of their caprices and the ridiculous vanity of their adorers. The Gankirō properly so called is the casino of the fashionable of Shin-Yoshiwara. Payment is made to the door-keeper on entering, and the visitor is introduced to the conversation room. Admirable order is preserved. Pipes and refreshments, such as are ordinarily given at all Japanese entertainments, are to be had in profusion to season the witty conversation of the ladies, one of whom undertakes to guide the visitor through the gardens and the various rooms. Every amusement has its tariff. In one of these rooms a vocal and instrumental concert will be going on, in another, character dances—both executed by women, professional artists residing at Edo, who have nothing in common with the inhabitants of Shin-Yoshiwara. These performances, even from our point of view, would be by no means unworthy of the best company.

A banqueting hall in the Gankirō is very curiously decorated, the walls are hung with beautiful sketches, either in genre or in landscape, some in Chinese ink, others colored, but all painted on pieces of cardboard cut after the pattern of the different sorts of fans used in the far East. But the greatest curiosity of the Gankirō is its children's theater. All the actors are young girls from seven to thirteen years of age, whose education is confided to the retired courtesans of Shin-Yoshiwara. The latter teach their pupils reading, writing, arithmetic, singing, music, dancing, acting and declamation. Operettas, little fairy pieces, and costume ballets, are executed by these children with infinite grace and dexterity. It is doubtful whether these pieces are not superior in literary value to the vaudevilles, the comedies, and the dramatic proverbs played in schools in Europe. But the little theater is certainly superior to such things among ourselves in talent, vivacity, and charming childish poetry. The spectacle is very pretty and very interesting. And yet, at the same time, what can be more sad than to see the young girls of the Gankirō so carefully educated? The sight only supplies an additional protest against these horrible institutions.

From time to time in the midst of the nocturnal rejoicings, a terrible rumor of a bloody catastrophe is spread around, and suddenly reveals the real horrors of these hideous places. Sometimes an unfortunate woman has completed with her own hand the work of destruction disease had commenced. Sometimes a young man, having reached the end of his expedients, fearing rejection by his mistress because he has no more money, kills her, and himself, in the apartment he has taken for her.

Generally, the courtesans of high rank in this place know how to avoid the double scandal. There are many whose pride consists in the number of their victims. Several of the most celebrated openly avow their contempt for men and for human life, their love of gain and taste for expenditure. The dread Gigoko attributed to herself a Satanic power over the human race. The embroideries of her *kimono* represent scenes of hell, the great judge summoning before his tribunal souls laden with guilt, and the damned expiating their sins in cauldrons of boiling water, or clothed with the bodies of monstrous beasts.

Of a lower grade in the social hell of Shin-Yoshiwara are the regions frequented by the small traders and the *hatamoto*. Suicide through love is frequently committed. The lover kills himself because he is not rich enough to purchase his mistress, and she kills herself because she has sworn to be faithful to him.

I have seen on the stage at Yokohama a play representing the tragical end of a courtesan, whose tender declarations had been interpreted by a young *samurai* in another sense than that known in Yoshiwara. Deceived in his love, outraged in his honor, the furious lover strikes off the head of the faithless woman with one blow of his sword. The Japanese theater represents this scene with full detail. The bloody sword flashes, and the victim falls under the eyes of the spectators, the orchestra breaks out into an expression of horror by the combined effect of all its instruments. Suddenly silence ensues, and the hero of the piece turns toward the public to give a pathetic explanation of his reasons. At the same moment the machinist moves a trap in the front of the stage, and the bloody head appears within two paces of the murderer, as if it had rolled to his feet.

The Shin-Yoshiwara is closed against Europeans. But in the ports opened by treaty, the Japanese government has instituted, and provided with every possible facility, brothels accessible to natives and foreigners alike. Feminine servitude seems to present itself under the hardest conditions known to humanity in this wretched place. Imagination which may conceive the hell of Dante, might fail before the horror of the reality of such lives.

Matsuri

Each of the major shrines in the city of Edo has its *matsuri*, or annual patronal festival. But among them there are several that celebrate this festival only once in two years. The solemnities are generally interesting only to the quarter, the street, or the small group of faithful who contribute to the maintenance of the monastery. To this rule there are remarkable exceptions. Certain *matsuri* are in favor with one entire section of the city, such as Honjo. And others seem to enjoy an unlimited popularity with the whole of Edo.

These *matsuri*, as we may easily conceive, are far from having preserved patriotic elevation and the noble simplicity which distinguished them in the splendid days of the national *kami* worship. The mythical sense of the solemnity is lost, its moral signification has fallen into oblivion. The fairs and rejoicings which in earlier times were only the accessories of the festival have now become its principal object, or rather its only interest. Thus in our own countries we see how the religious festivals of the Middle Ages have disappeared, leaving behind their *kermesse*, or popular fair, which was developed year after year under their protection. So at Edo certain feasts recall the names of the ancient national divinities, the goddess of the sun, the god of the moon, the god of water, the patron of rice, the god of the sea, the god of war, whose anniversary is celebrated on the first day of the second month, corresponding to our March. But the chief characteristic of these solemnities is the theatrical pomp displayed in them, in the processions and the choirs of music—the dances and the pantomimes of the priests on the one hand, and the masquerades and scenic representations in the open air on the other. In addition to these attractions, there are illuminations, public games, archery, horse racing, wrestling, public lotteries, and everywhere a market of fruit and fish according to the season, pastry, sweetmeats, flowers, articles in common use—such as fans, umbrellas, paper lanterns, and children's toys.

The subject of the *matsuri* in a city like Edo, where the temples and shrines are counted by hundreds, is impossible to treat in minute detail. I can only give a few rapid sketches of those festivals that excite general attention, and attract the entire population of the city to their scenes.

On the fifth day of the fifth month, the crowd repairs in the early morning to the woods of the suburb of Fuchū for the Kurayami *matsuri*, and gather herbs whose virtue is held to be sovereign in cases of contagious maladies. An improvised fair on the border of the forest enables the pilgrims to provide themselves with everything they will require during the day. In the evening the priests of the Ōkunitama shrine in the neighborhood proceed to the annual purification of the holy place. While the shrine is being cleaned, a solemn procession marches through the woods during the greater part of the night, carrying relics belonging to the sanctuary. Piles of resinous wood are prepared in the court of the sacred enclosure, at the foot of the *torii* in the avenue, and at the openings of the forest paths at their diverging points, and all along the road the cortege is to take. At a given signal, all these are lighted at once, and the procession sets out, having been provided with abundant paper lanterns of various colors, and accompanied by the music of fifes, gongs, and the big drums of the shrine. From every side a crowd accumulates on the route of the procession, uttering cries, which are echoed by thousands of startled birds disturbed from their sleep by the strange light and clamor.

At the head of the procession, immediately after the band, march the horses of the *kami*, led by the bridle by grooms attired in an antique national costume. They are followed by the high priests and their acolytes and servants, carrying the sacred arms, trophies of the ancient heroes. Then, preceded by the *gohei*, or antique holy water brush, come two personages, who wear masks representing heads of Korean dogs. They are followed by the entire body of priests and their servants, who are charged with the care of *mikoshi*, the furniture, and the utensils of the shrine and its dependencies. When the cortage has passed through all the exterior stations, it returns to the sacred place, and the flames are extinguished, the crowd disperses to the restaurants in the fair and on the roadside, darkness and silence take possession of the forest.

On the twenty-fourth day of the eighth month, the fraternity of the shrine of Tenmangu, in Honjo, which is purified on the twenty-fifth day of the second month, exhibits the image of its god, which is drawn through the principal streets of Edo on an oxcart. The chief officers of the families who patronize this shrine, and the priests who serve in the shrine, precede and follow the car, accompanied, by coolies carrying coffers and baskets, which contain the utensils and sacred objects belonging to the shrine.

In the great biennial procession of the shrine of Kanda Myōjin, which is placed under the invocation of Kanda the patron of Edo, there is a whole cavalcade of historical personages, among whom the *shōgun* is especially distinguished. In order to add to the effect of this procession, the monks invite a certain number of courtesans, who are carried in elegant palanquins. The car of the saint of Myōjin is drawn by two oxen, and by an unlimited number of the faithful, voluntarily harnessed to the sacred vehicle by straw ropes. A few feet behind it a hideous colossal head of the demon over whom the saint triumphed is carried on a platform. The people contemplate with horror the gigantic horns and erect crest of this monster, they point out to one another its bloody eyes, its scarlet skin and horrible jaws. To add to the effect of this spectacle, the priests blow through their conch shells, producing a terrible noise. A little further on an enormous axe, with which the victorious hero cut off the monsters head, is exhibited.

But all the united wonders of the procession of Myōjin fade before the splendor of the festival given annually by the priests of the Sannō Hiei shrine, which is sacred to the memory of Emperor Jinmu, the founder of the empire of the great Japan. This is the most imposing of the *matsuri* of Edo. It takes place on the fifteenth day of the sixth month. Tengu, the faithful porter and messenger of the gods, heads the procession, adorned in his brilliant costume as the celestial herald. He half unfolds a pair of iris colored wings. His smiling air, his cunning eyes, his crimson color, his nose of preposterous length, excite merriment in the people, and secure the warmest welcome for the cortege. When the evil spirits find the image of Tengu at the door of the shrines of the national religion, they hasten on. The procession has therefore nothing to dread from them.

The municipal police is charged with the maintenance of public order. More than a million of spectators preserve perfect discipline during the whole of this great day. In all the streets and all the squares through which the procession is to pass, platforms are erected for the women, old men, and children. Places are reserved for those who choose to pay for them, free space is assigned to the workmen, but everybody is bound to remain quietly in his place during the entire festival. Only the sellers of fruit, cakes, and *sake*, have permission to go beyond the boundary rope that separates the crowd from the road kept for the procession.

The procession of Sannō is a kind of national encyclopaedia in action, in which we find all sorts of historical lessons, mythological symbols, traditions, and popular actions mixed up together, just as we see Bacchus, Silenus, Noah's Ark, Ceres, and Pomona, introduced indiscriminately in the old festival of the vine dressers at Vevy. When art attains this democratic breadth, criticism must merely bow and be silent.

I pass on to the most picturesque details of the ceremony. Here comes the patron of the sacred dance of the Dairi. The image, dressed in the old theatrical garments of Kyoto, is raised on a huge drum, supported by figurants in costumes of festive form and crowns of flowers. This is followed by the procession of the white elephant. The animal is made of cardboard, and its bearers are skilfully hidden in its capacious body, their feet are hardly seen moving under the legs of the colossus, which is preceded by a band of music, composed of flutes, trumpets, big drums, cymbals, gongs, and tambourines. The men of this group wear beards, a painted hat with an aigrette, boots, a long robe with a wide girdle, and some of them carry Chinese banners covered with images of dragons. A little further on a gigantic lobster is carried by a priest of the *kami* worship, and surrounded by a troop of negroes.

Then come a hundred cultivators who are harnessed to the chariot of the ox, this king of domestic animals is placed on the vehicle under the shade of a flowering peach tree, and is accompanied by the demi-god who introduced him into Japan. Six other chariots are laden with picturesque trophies formed of the implements and products of rice culture.

A cortege of Shintō priests generally forms a guard of honor to a carriage made in the likeness of that of the emperor, a splendid chariot, surmounted

by the sacred gong and the cock of the Dairi. Antique banners, some ornamented by sketches of horses, precede a cavalcade of superior officers
costumed according to the court fashions of Kyoto. Suddenly two terrible
monsters appear, they have the face of the tiger with the horns of a bull.
Their great tails are elevated high above the helmets of the men-at-arms
who surround them. Perhaps they recall under a fantastic form the memory
of those tigers who gave so much trouble to the soldiers of the heroic mother
of Hachiman in the Korean fields. To this group belongs the exhibition of
the antique arms of the arsenal of Sannō Hiei shrine, lances and halberds,
two-handed swords, bows, arrows, war fans and insignia of command. By
degrees the exhibition loses its warlike character, in their turn appear priests
and attendants, carrying the *mikoshi*, the vases of the sanctuary, and all the
furniture of the shrine and its dependencies under banners covered with
hieroglyphic signs. Another troop of attendants carries paper lanterns at
the end of long poles. Among the banners we recognize that of the quarter
of Shin-Yoshiwara. This very effective group terminates the procession.

Then come seven of the handsomest women in this reserved portion of
the capital, majestically attired in state costume, each is accompanied by
her waiting woman and by an attendant who carries a wide and lofty parasol,
which shades her from the rays of the sun. Her headdress is two or three
storeys high, and the edifice is supported by large pins of red tortoiseshell.
Her face shines with cosmetics carefully applied. We may count the number
of her robes—thanks to five or six collars hanging over her shoulders. A
wide *kimono* envelops her and sweeps the ground, its folds are slightly raised
by means of an enormous girdle composed of an entire piece of silk or
velvet. And some inches are added to her already noble stature by the curious
manner in which she is shod with little planks of wood.

These seven figurants are well known to all the people. As they pass, their
names are mentioned on all sides, and indeed these names are embroidered
on their rich costume. The first is the Lady of the War Fan, which she displays
on her wide velvet sash, her robe is embroidered with four cocks of various
plumage, two of which are white, worked on the ample sleeves of her
kimono, the silken feathers of their tails wave gracefully in the air with each
of her movements. The second is the Lady of the Golden Fish. She wears
one on each side of her robe on a background of waves and foam in silver

thread. The accessory embroideries represent little children playing with ribbons of all sorts of colors, who sport on her *kimono*. Need I speak of the lady of the Death's head, the Lady of the Candelabra, the Lady of the Slaves, the Lady of the Chrysanthemums? No! For where should I stop if I were to describe in all its details the public homage paid to the courtesans by the priests and by the people of Edo In the presence of such customs we can only admire the appropriateness with which the great Sannō admits to the rank of its idols and solemnly exhibits in the streets of the city, a monkey, with a red face, wearing a sacerdotal mitre, and carrying a holy water brush. That mocking image mounted on a drum, with rich drapery, is lifted high above the crowd, an ironical caricature of the religious exhibition which the crowd just witness.

The *matsuri* of the shrines of Japan do the government of that country a service by absolving it from the charge of amusing its subjects, who supply all funds needful for the purpose out of their own pockets. There are Japanese festivals that do not consist of representations and amusements given by the priests to the people but of real public rejoicings, in which the people themselves are the only actors and the real heroes of the day.

These are the five great annual festivals. They had originally a religious stamp, which did not actually militate against the gaiety of their exterior manifestations, because the moral of the *kami* worship is, that a joyous heart is integrally in a state of purity. The festival of the first day of the first month is naturally the chief festival of the new year. It is that of visits, of congratulations and presents, the latter consisting of at least two or three fans, which the visitor brings, according to custom, in a box of lacquer tied with silken cords. No matter what the nature or the value of the principal gift, it is always accompanied by a screw of paper containing a dried morsel of the flesh of the shellfish named *awabi*, or of the *ebi*, an exceedingly common fish. And this manifestation is a piece of homage paid to the frugality of the antique national customs. The family receiving the visit gives a little collation composed of *sake*, rice bread, and mandarin oranges. The lobster plays an important part in the exchange of presents. Every house religiously preserves one until the following year, unless it should be required as a remedy against certain maladies, in which case it is ground to powder and eaten.

The second of the five festivals, the Feast of Dolls, takes place on the third day of the third month. I witnessed it at Nagasaki on the 20th of April, 1863. It is consecrated to feminine youth. The mother of the family adorns the guest chamber with branches of the flowering peach, and there lays out an exhibition of the dolls her children received at their birth. These are very pretty and elegantly dressed, representing the emperor, the empress, and other personages of the imperial court. The offering is made complete by a feast, which is prepared by the young girls who are old enough to do so, and towards evening the viands are eaten by the company.

On the fifth day of the fifth month a festival of a less domestic character, called Festival of the Banners, is celebrated in honor of the boys. Edo is on this day a charming spectacle, especially when contemplated from a gallery looking on one of the wide streets of the city, which is decked out from early morning with tall bamboos surmounted with plumes, or waving horse-tails, or balls of gilded paper, and with long floating banners of painted paper, fish made of lacquer or of plaited straw, and above all, with great banners stretched on reed frames, and adorned with armorial bearings, family names, patriotic sentences or heroic figures. The bronze workshops exhibit casques, sets of complete armour, and gigantic halberds of fantastic forms. Groups of boys in full dress occupy the public roads, some wearing two small swords, similar to those of the *yakunin*, at their girdle, others with fine paper ribbons on their shoulders carry an immense wooden sword ornamented with various colors, and others bear small flags, which reproduce the favorite subjects of the street banners.

The fourth great annual feast, that of the seventh day of the seventh month, is known under the name of the Festival of Lanterns. Little girls parade the illuminated streets of the city of Edo in great numbers, singing with all their heart, and swinging paper lanterns. In certain cities of the south the population visit the hill cemeteries and pass the night amid the tombs.

The thirteenth, fourteenth, and fifteenth are the days on which every one goes to the temples to pray for the dead and to burn candles for them, the fifteenth being the day fixed for the regulation of accounts for the first half of the year. The public rejoicings which succeed the fulfilment of this troublesome duty are particularly varied and brilliant. Masquerades, accompanied by national dances, take a high place among the popular pleasures.

All the masks have their signification and traditional character. There are the noble types, first the placid faces of the gentlemen and ladies of the Dairi, then the fierce physiognomies of the heroes of the civil wars. There are also masks with moveable jaws, in imitation of those worn by the emperor's actors. Others represent the grotesque and divine Tengu, the good Okame, the jolliest of the Japanese women mentioned in history, or the unhappy Hyottoko, the ideal of ugliness. These masks reproduce all the varieties of the race of demons—those with one eye, with two eyes, with three and four eyes, with horns and without horns, with two or even three horns, from the sprites to the giants, and even to the odious Hannya, the feminine devil. The final category includes masks made in the likeness of the fox, the monkey, or the Korean lion, or of the *kappa*, the man-frog who haunts the shores of Japan. The dances are of every conceivable description, the rice dance alone numbers thirty figures, executed by men whose entire clothing consists of a girdle of rice straw, a round hat of the same material brought down over their eyes, and a small cloak with large sleeves imitating the wings of nocturnal moths.

The fifth of the five festivals falls on the ninth day of the ninth month. This is the Feast of Chrysanthemums. In all family repasts leaves of these beautiful flowers are scattered on cups of tea or the bowls of *sake*. Libations prepared in this fashion are supposed to prolong life. The citizen of Edo would believe that he had failed in his duty as a husband and father if he drank only moderately of this precious drink.

Among the festivals of the fourth month, the eighth day is sacred to the baptism of Buddha as he is represented at his birth, standing, pointing one hand to heaven and the other hand to earth. Not only do his devotees bathe with consecrated tea the bronze image of the holy child in the places that serve for fonts in the Buddhist temples, but the attendants of the monasteries go through the streets carrying his statuette fixed in the centre of a tub, so that the same ceremony may take place in private houses, such solicitude brings them in a considerable reward.

The festivals of the sixth month are in honor of the cereal harvest—rice, millet, wheat, and paddy. The priests bless little squares of white paper fastened to sticks, which the cultivators buy and plant at the four corners of their fields, under the persuasion that these rustic amulets are indispensable to the fruitfulness of the soil. This season of the year is a time of rejoicing for the citizens of Edo, who assemble in the shady groves on the shores of the Sumida-*gawa*, or in the gardens of Ōji, under green arbors moistened with the foam of the cascades, or crowd the boats on the great river, until the last day of the month convokes them to solemn expiation and general purification.

The god of the water, an ancient divinity of the *kami* worship, is feted from one end to the other of the empire during the whole of the seventh month, which represents the entire term of the rainy season. Bamboos, from whose upper branches glass bells and strips of blessed paper are suspended, are planted beside the springs, the wells and the irrigating channels. And every morning and evening banners are waved inscribed with this sentence, "Respect and homage to the God of the Water." In the houses of the country people offerings, consisting of rice, fish, and small money, are made on the domestic altar of the *kami*.

The eighth month commences by a ceremonious exchange of civilities between clients and their patrons, employes and their chiefs, subalterns and their superiors.

The fifteenth day is dedicated to the god of the moon. It is said to be the moment of the year in which the orb of night emits its utmost brilliancy. The rivers and canals are crowded with gondolas, from which the citizens contemplate the full moon. The stillness of the air and the warmth of the temperature during the evenings of the months of September and October are favorable to these nocturnal parties of pleasure, also to those taking place in the public gardens of the city and its suburbs.

The tenth month is placed under the invocation of Ebisu, who is at once the god of fishing and one of the favorite patrons of the shopkeepers, who make each other presents on this occasion, among which are millet-cakes and a large red fish named *tai* (red snapper), much admired for its beauty and the delicacy of its flavor.

The ladies of Edo are not less diligent in the performance of the duties imposed on them by their social position. They pay each other neighborly visits, and do not neglect to burn candles before the image of Ebisu for the prosperity of their husbands' commercial enterprises. Early in the morning they may be seen going in groups to certain shrines, in whose sanctuaries there are altars privileged to receive the homage of the female citizens. To perform this ceremony the pilgrim is attired in a headdress, consisting of a cotton handkerchief of dazzling whiteness, artistically wound through the thick hair.

Towards the middle of the month everyone is bound to notice and to communicate to his friends the fact that the leaves of the maple trees are beginning to change color. At the commencement of the eleventh, month the maple is in all the magnificence of its autumn dress. Crowds assemble in the gardens of the monasteries and the teahouses. With the winter solstice come general congratulations. This is the Festival of Matrons. No pressure of business, no journey to the city, no cause or pretext whatever, can on this occasion excuse the absence of the husbands from their homes. They come from all parts of the country, and in the evening the city is illuminated on all sides. The sounds of guitars and joyous voices fill the air on this universal festival.

The fifteenth day is called the Passing of the River, by reason of a religious domestic solemnity, it symbolizes the flight of time, and the transition to the new year.

The twelfth month is devoted to the settlement of affairs, the renewal of furniture, and the rearrangement of the household, operations which involve such a succession of ceremonies, formalities, festivals, and rejoicings, that a whole volume might be written on the four or five weeks at the end of January and the commencement of February in the cities and the villages of Japan.

Theater

Although the great dramatic system of modern Japan, the theater, or *shibai*, is far from being an aristocratic institution, it is one of the most curious in the world. If it does not attain to the distinguished literary merit of Chinese drama, or to the perfection of acting, it far exceeds both in poetic value, because it has more simplicity, more passion, more individuality and a more purely human character. In China, the public look on at the piece and criticize the actors; in Japan, the public take part in the piece in concert with the actors, exchange sentiments with them, and, in fact, are part of the spectacle. In this respect the theater reminds us of the little day-theaters of Italy, but with all the difference that exists between an amusing and easy recreation and a great popular subject, confused, often unintelligible, and whose gaiety is strange and fantastic. Although the *shibai* is implanted in all the cities of Japan, it is at Edo, and especially in the city and the northern departments, that it is most active and important. The theaters are exceedingly numerous, one group occupying three longitudinal and four cross streets.

The dramatic authors of Edo write principally for these theaters. From there, new pieces are distributed throughout the empire, and companies of comedians from the capital take, like the wrestlers, their holidays in the provinces. The actors are all male. Only female dancers appear on the boards, and then in the ballet of the Grand Opera only. Comedians form a separate class, who are regarded by the higher orders with contempt. The *shibai* is, properly speaking, the theater of the middle classes of the Japanese population. It attracts great numbers of coolies and laborers, when they can afford to go, but all classes above the traders abstain from dramatic representations, or, if they go, take care to sit in latticed boxes. Among the crowds that frequent the theatrical district it is extremely rare to meet two-sworded men—not that the *samurai* are not sometimes mixed up with the people, but they take good care to disguise themselves on this and other compromising occasions. Just before sunset certain delegates from the company of actors appear on platforms raised on the right and left of the doors of the theaters, they are in ordinary dress, and harangue the multitude, explaining the subject of the pieces about to be performed, and the merit of the principal actors who perform in them.

After this exordium come familiar jokes, pleasant talking, the eloquence of mimicry, and the high art of managing the fan. Presently the lanterns are lit. "Come in, gentlemen! come in, ladies!" they cry, "take your places! now's the time! the piece is about to begin." Nevertheless, nobody is in a hurry, for the spectacle in the street captivates general attention. The illuminations afford great pleasure to the people. The first row of red lanterns hangs all along the whole length of the roof. A little lower is a second range under the roof. Between the two hang balls of transparent paper, each containing a painted candle. Near the doors enormous oblong lanterns light up the pictures and the inscriptions, illustrating the principal subjects and scenes of the pieces. Every theater has its own arms and its own colors painted on banners and lanterns, along three sides of a sort of belvedere or square tower that springs from the roof.

The buildings adjoining those of the *shibai* are occupied by restaurants, and are as gaily decorated as the exterior of the theater, with designs and carvings which have some relation to the name of each of these establishments. One is the restaurant of Fuji-*yama*, and another of the Rising Sun, farther off we see those of the Tori, the Tai Fish, the Merchant Junk, the Stork, the Two Lovers, etc., etc. But it is time to go into the theater, and we ascend a wooden staircase leading to the second gallery. A functionary opens a spacious box, and a servant brings *sake*, tea, cakes, sweetmeats, and pipes and tobacco.

The interior of the theater forms a long square. There are two ranges of galleries, the upper containing the best places in the theater. Numbers of ladies are to be seen there in full dress—ladies, that is to say, covered up to their eyes in crape dresses and silk mantles. The whole of the remainder of the house is occupied exclusively by men. There is no orchestra. The floor of the house, as seen from a distance, resembles a draughtboard. It is divided into compartments, containing from eight to twelve places each, most of which are hired by the year by the citizens, who take their children regularly to the play. There are no lobbies. Everyone walks to his or her place on the planks enclosing the compartments at the height of the spectators' shoulders, who squat on their heels or crouch on little stools. There is neither a ladder nor a staircase by which to get down into the midst of them. The men hold out their arms to the women and children.

The settling of the audience in its place forms a very picturesque part in the preliminaries of the performance. Tobacco and refreshments are served during the whole evening by attendants and servants, by the same means of communication. On both sides of the pit are two bridges of planks, which also communicate with the boards of the stage, the first is nearest to one of the doors, the second, which is four planks wide, forms an angle with the extremity of the boxes. On this bridge certain heroic or tragi-comic personages perform their parts, and the ballet is danced.

The house is lit by paper lanterns tied to the galleries, there is no chandelier from the roof, which is perfectly flat, the cupola being unknown in Japanese architecture. I have seen large lanterns held up to the roof of a theater at Yokohama in order to light up the performance of the acrobats, especially that of the flying men, who cross the theater by means of cleverly contrived mechanism.

The curtain that hangs before the stage is ornamented by a gigantic inscription in Chinese characters, and surmounted by a target with an arrow in the centre. This symbolical sign is supposed to be a prognostic of the talent about to be displayed by the actors, and which will hit the bull's-eye in the hearts of their audience. The performance generally lasts until one o'clock in the morning. It consists of a comedy, a tragedy, an opera with a ballet, and two or three interludes of acrobats, wrestlers, and jugglers. The principal parts are announced by a clicking noise, produced by striking a small piece of wood against the floor of the stage. The appearance of infernal personages is always preceded by lightning. The actors worthy of particular notice are escorted by one or two attendants, who carry a long stick, at the end of which is a little candlestick with a lighted candle. The spectators have only to follow the combined movement of the two lights to know exactly what they ought to admire, sometimes it is the expression of the actor's face, sometimes his attitude and gesture, and sometimes the details of his costume and headdress.

The same custom prevails with regard to the dancers. The attendants may be seen during the ballet squatting on the bridge I have described, and profiting by the immediate neighborhood of the spectators to get them to snuff the candles with their fingers, an office they always perform with pleasure. It would indeed be impossible to find anywhere a more good-humored audience. In homely comedies the spectators frequently interrupt the actors, and answer them. Thus audience and actors contribute alike to the success of the evening and the satisfaction of all concerned. The zeal and contentment of the public are manifested by their gifts, in addition to the price paid for admission. Almost every theater displays innumerable scraps of paper fastened to the walls by which artists relate acts of generosity, and record the name and address of their benefactors.

We cannot yet form an appreciation of Japanese drama from a literary point of view. No piece has been translated into any European language. Sir Rutherford Alcock gives a detailed analysis of a performance he witnessed at Osaka. In comparing my own observations with his and those of Layrle, I have come to the conclusion that dramatic art is still in its infancy in modern Japan. The political circumstances of the country render historical drama impossible. The nearest approach to it in the repertory of the *shibai* is an incongruous mixture of history, mythology, and burlesque.

Opera, less advanced even than drama, is very much inferior to that of China, and imitates it only on its most fanciful side, the marvels of the Buddhist demonology. Comedy seems to promise well, because it observes the conditions of the natural and the real. It admits, no doubt, like opera, of scenes of incredible coarseness. Nevertheless, nothing appears more immoral to the Japanese than our drama. This apparent contradiction is easily explained. Japanese realism admits on the stage, as in romance, types and situations of which *La Dame aux Camélias*, *La Fille de marbre*, and all our licentious literature, gives only a feeble idea. On the other hand, it absolutely excludes every intrigue by which the character of a married woman is compromised. Neither Phsedra, nor Hamlet's mother, the husbands depicted by Molière, nor Werther, nor Charlotte, nor the infamous Madame Bovary, could have offered the slightest attraction for the imagination of the Japanese.

The green rooms and the side-scenes of the theaters of the Far East are no less interesting to the foreign observer than the theater, properly so called, and the audience that crowds it. In these places none but men are to be seen, excepting from time to time some servants, or the artists' wives who bring refreshments to their husbands, or come to give the last touch to their toilet before they go on the stage in the costume of either sex. In the midst of the general disorder we find some very characteristic groups. Here are musicians occupied in refreshing themselves, and indifferent to everything else until the signal to return to their posts reaches them; there two actors are rehearsing together the attitude and gesture which in a few minutes are to delight the spectators. And another, sitting on his heels before a looking-glass placed on the floor, is painting his face and adjusting his feminine headdress. A young devil beside him has thrown back his mask, with its horns and its mane, over his shoulders, and is fanning himself, while the chief of the wrestlers is tranquilly smoking his pipe in the midst of the acrobats. Among the crowd, carpenters are coming and going, carrying the screens and the partitions destined for the change of scene, the machinist is working a trap through which a whirlwind of flame is about to escape. And the piece is going on outside to the accompaniment of drum-beating, amid the conversation of the public in the house and that of the disengaged actors.

In the restaurant there is apparent inextricable confusion. Everyone crouches on his mat, except the servants. All sorts of games are in progress, and *sake* is circulating freely. Sometimes a group of dancers install themselves round the domestic altar under the image of the god of contentment. They seldom fail by their guitars and their voices to arouse the enthusiasm of some young dandy, who will forsake his party, advance towards the performers, and execute under their fair eyes a very elegant dance to the accompaniment of the solemn motion of his fan. The restaurant supplies all the deficiencies of the theater in point of refreshment, and is frequently crowded during the greater part of the piece. Everybody knows all about it, and does not mind sacrificing a few scenes to the pleasures of the table.

Bakumatsu Japan

The so-called spectators will eat and drink at the restaurant until the gong gives the signal for the great interlude of the jugglers. Then the restaurant changes its aspect completely, everyone hastens to his place in the theater.

The Suburbs

Nothing gives such an idea of the immense circumference of Edo than following the outer zone of the quarters situated on the south, the west, and north of the citadel, for it extends from the suburb of Shinagawa, opposite the six forts of the bay, and the country traversed by the northern road beyond the bridge of Senju Ōhashi. It embraces on the north of Honda those fertile fields that are watered on one side by the Sumida-*gawa*, and on the other by Ara-*kawa*, the small river that forms the eastern boundary of the three districts on the right bank. A description of the quarters comprised in this suburb would be tiresome, because they have all a uniform agglomerate character, and the curiosities they contain are all of the same kind, sometimes rustic temples built on the funeral hills, sometimes granite statues or commemorative tables raised on the tomb of some celebrated personage, and destined to perpetuate the remembrance of a remarkable event in the history of the ancient *shōgun*. Here are teahouses, great orchards, horticultural establishments; there are sacred trees, wayside alters set up at the best points of view, and sometimes an isolated hill, cut in the shape of Fuji-*yama*.

Seen from a birdseye view, these outer suburbs look like a park, or a continuous garden dotted with rural habitations. Or it resembles a garland of verdure and flowers, cast round the suburbs of the south and the districts of the west, and uniting them to the artizan's quarters, in the heart of the city and to the villages that extend to the rice fields.

When the orchards are in flower, the citizen, the painter, and the student, are seized with rural fancies—they fly from the labours and the pleasures of the capital, and hide themselves for a day, or for many days, if it be possible, among the rustic roofs of the teahouses. These charming retreats, rich with the beauties of nature, are innumerable. Most of them can hardly be distinguished from the country houses in their neighborhood. Their vast roofs come down to the ground floor. Domestic birds flutter, or plume themselves in the sun, on the moss with which the roof is covered, and that rises to the summit, where we see long lines of iris in full flower. When there is no gallery, arbors of vines, or other climbing plants, shelter the guests grouped negligently on the threshold. A limpid spring murmurs and flows along the path, which descends towards the plain across the gardens and vineyards, the poppy and bean fields, or the great expanse of cereal and textile plants.

In February, in June, and in October, three times a year, certain societies accomplish a rural pilgrimage into the villages at three or four miles distant from Edo, merely to behold with their own eyes the vicissitudes of the seasons and the transformations of nature.

In winter, if the snow should fall, it is considered a duty as well as a pleasure that whole families should go and contemplate the strange aspect of the statues in the enclosure of the Kanda Myōjin, in the high pagoda of Asakusa. But above all, no one must fail to retire to certain teahouses in the suburbs, such as those of Niken Chaya, in the neighborhood of Fukagawa, to admire the spectacle of the bay and the country under the novel decoration. In summer, it is agreed that the concert of grasshoppers must be listened to on the heights of Dokan-*yama*. A good family man would never fail to take his children there, plentifully supplied with little wicker cages, in order to bring back some of these sweet songsters.

Poets of the spring, choristers of the summer, painters and artists who seek for new inspirations, delight to abandon themselves from morning to evening to charming study and reverie among the orchards of cherry, plum, pear, and peach trees, among the groves of bamboo, citrons, oranges, pines, and cypress, which surround the temples, the gardens of the teahouses of Okanbo, Sugamo, Itabashi, Negishi, Haghitera, Mimeguri, and a multitude of other classic retreats of the muses of Japan. When night has come they meet in excellent inns, and combine with the pleasures of the table the enjoyment of society, where conversation alternates with songs and music, and drawings are exhibited in exchange for pages of poetry which have been written during the day.

The pencil often intervenes in the capricious conversation, and the subject of a tale or a discussion is illustrated or travestied by the imagination of the painter amid the applause of the company.

Japanese caricatures generally bear the impress of good nature. They are, for the most part, taken from middle-class life. A grave physician is studying the state of his patient's tongue, or examining with a vain expenditure of spectacles the ailing eyes—he is lifting up the corner of the eyelid with great care. Quacks are engaged in the massaging or in the application of *moxa*, a band of blind masseurs on their travels have gone astray at a ford, and are disputing in the midst of the water as to the direction which they should take on reaching the opposite bank. Then we have types of the begging friars, of fishing misadventures, scenes of feminine jealousy and household quarrels pushed to violent measures. There are also very complete series of caricatures, such as the small troubles of life in the great world, the household of the fat man, and the household of the thin man. And the different grimaces that can be formed by the human face. The artists do not spare themselves. For rapid painting, which is held in such esteem in Japan, is symbolized under the figure of an artist who is working with six brushes at once, two in each hand and one between each great toe.

The method that rendered Jean-Jacques Grandville so popular in his illustration of the fables of Jean de La Fontaine is not unknown to Japanese caricaturists. But their pencil is less sparing, they only exceptionally reach to the dramatic energy of the human passions. Most frequently they limit themselves to giving animals a costume, or an attitude that invests them with a certain symbolic character. This is the lower degree of anthropomorphism. Such for example is the personification of the twelve signs of the Zodiac—the mouse, the bear, the tiger, the hare, the dragon, the serpent, the horse, the ram, the monkey, the cock, the dog, and the wild boar—each adorned with vestments and attributes relating to their astronomical functions, or to the parts they play in astrology.

A sketch by Hokusai, no less harmless, but more amusing, represents a rice warehouse in which rats, the most dreaded enemies of that precious cereal, form the warehousemen. Nothing is missing in this pretty scene, from the cashier making his calculations with his bead frame, to the salesman turning over his books in order to demonstrate to a purchaser that he cannot abate a farthing in the price. The shopmen are carrying the bales, of which the purchaser is taking an invoice, on their shoulders. The money is in little straw bags, which the coolies carry at the ends of their bamboos. Everything is conducted with the order and regularity becoming to a great house. The smallest details are drawn with the care that would be bestowed on a serious composition. It is in this kind of comic art, childish or heroic by turns, that the Japanese display most ease and originality.

I frequently noticed a dash of satire of a political kind in the numerous and varied sketches whose subject is furnished by the trains of the *daimyō*. For instance, I have seen many in which the personages of the cortege, beginning with the *daimyō* himself, are represented as foxes or monkeys. The satirical intention is not less manifest in those pictures in which we see the superior of a monastery with a wolf's head, and a group of nuns under the image of weasels. The most expressive picture I have seen of this kind represents an audience in which a hare has prostrated himself, trembling, at the feet of a wild boar. The hare is a little *hatamoto* out of employment, and the wild boar is a high-class functionary in court dress, who wears the toque of Kyoto.

The taste for the fantastic goes along with that for caricature. In Japan, political institutions, religion, and nature, all concur to excite the imagination and to set it wandering to the region of chimeras. On the sea-shore, the basalt rocks take forms now grotesque and now frightful. The ocean itself is a world of mysteries. Sometimes, when it is very dark, a light may be seen under the water resembling a dragon. Sailors have seen shells darting along among the waves. Under the waters of the Strait of Shimonoseki is a grotto, or rather a temple, encrusted with pearls and mother-of-pearl. It is called the Ryōgon. It is situated in the place where the young emperor Antoku was submerged with his suite as he fled from the field of battle where his partisans, the Heike, were defeated by Minamoto Yoritomo (1185). In this temple he reigns and holds his court. His men-at-arms carry long rods surmounted by sharks' fins, these are his banners. All the sea gods, wearing diadems representing the heads of seals, little fishes, medusas, crabs, and dragon's jaws, come to pay him homage. This court of marine monsters and drowned men-at-arms has inspired the strangest artistic compositions, equalled only by the revolting scenes in which we see the blood and slaughtered victims aiding demons in the punishment of their murderers in the infernal regions. The pencil of Jacques Callot has produced nothing so completely horrible.

The Japanese delight in the imitation of hideous realities. The wax-work museum at Asakusa-*dera* houses figures of executed criminals, and corpses in a state of decomposition, which form a collection very superior to the celebrated Chamber of Horrors at Madame Tussauds. They can also, like Callot, ally the burlesque to the horrible, but they do so only in subjects that are not tragical. For instance, they will change the vessels used in religious ceremonies, gongs, holy water brushes, candelabra, perfume vases, altars, images, and statuettes, into so many animated monsters, jumping or crawling in an infernal dance led by evil spirits.

The fantastic has its part in the fascinations of the teahouses in the suburbs of Edo. Some are erected in places propitious to the contemplation of Fuji-*yama*, and the sight of that extraordinary mountain as it appears at sunrise or at sunset under the clear sky, or when swept by storms, is such as to satisfy the most exacting imagination. The charm of the landscape and mysterious cataracts forming cascades, is enhanced in other places by mineral springs and basins of thermal water, like certain watering places in the Swiss mountains. People do not go there for the purpose of cure, but they go to pass a few days with their families in elegant cedar chalets shaded with magnificent trees, on the banks of the water-course, which may be compared to the finest Alpine rivers. The most frequented are those of Otonashi-*gawa*, one of the principal tributaries of the great river.

Other places of pleasure are specially devoted to one or other of the popular superstitions. The people go from the temples to the teahouses with the satisfaction that accompanies the accomplishment of a pious task. During the first days of the eleventh month the hotel keepers and the monks of the Yushima Tenjin shrine receive thousands of pilgrims of both sexes, small traders, and agriculturists, in the suburbs or the country immediately around the city, who come to buy rakes at an isolated temple in a marsh on the north of the capital. These rakes are of good augury for harvest, and are simply pious playthings, which are held as talismans in the dwellings of the faithful. They suit all purses and the most varied tastes. Some—of colossal size—are decorated with a picture, representing the junk of happiness; others—of smaller dimensions—are ornamented with the sign of the god of riches, the simplest have only pictures on paper or on *papier mâché*, such as the head of the god of rice, the mask of Okara, and all sorts of mythological emblems. As fortune does not confer its favors among men in proportion to their stature, it frequently happens that, on their return from the Yushima Tenjin shrine, the poorest pilgrims carry away the thinnest loads, while their companions, rich but feeble, stagger under the weight of the enormous instruments their social position has obliged them to purchase.

The comic effect of the procession is increased by the peculiarities of the costumes of the season. The men wear tight trousers of blue cotton and a wide mantle with large sleeves, they are mostly bareheaded, but their noses are protected by crape handkerchiefs tied at the back of the neck, others cover the head with an ample hood, which hides the whole face with the exception of the eyes. The women generally adopt this ugly hood, and, stuff their arms into the thick sleeves of their winter *kimono*, so that they look as if they had none. Amulets to be placed at the edges of the fields, in the form of squares of paper fixed on a wooden peg, are sold at the Yushima Tenjin shrine. And the bareheaded pilgrims stick them behind the one plait of hair forming their headdress, like hairpins, so that they look as if they had come from an agricultural exhibition with the number under which they were exhibited stuck on their head.

On the other side of the Sumida-*gawa* the cultivation of trees used in manufactures occupies a no less important place among the labours of the country people than the culture of the rice fields and their kitchen garden. Among others we may see great plantations of poison sumach and paper mulbery, which supply the dye and paper fabrics of the capital. The former of these shrubs acquires in about thirteen years an annual value of from £3 to £4, the sap is taken away twice, by means of incisions made in January and renewed in September. The dye produced in the latter month is of inferior quality. In order to avoid cantact of the skin with the native dye, which possesses venomous properties, the workpeople cover their hands and face with a thick coating of oil.

On the right bank of the river, and on the shores of its principal affluents, the builders and master-carpenters of Edo have their timberyards, where the trunks of trees brought from the forests of the interior are cut into beams, laths, and planks. These forests are inexhaustibly rich in woods fit for building purposes, such as the oak, which attains an immense height in Japan, the pine, of which some forty species exist, the cedar, Cryptomeria, of a native species, the fir tree, also remarkable for its variety. And the brown woods, and black employed in cabinet making or in small ornaments.

The Gardens of the Ōji Inari shrine, which stand high in the estimate of the city population, are situate at the opening of a mountain gorge on the northern side of Edo. A small river forming several cascades winds gracefully through the valley. On the bank above its limpid waters, rises the long galleries and pavilions of the teahouse, which enjoys the coolness of the water and the shade of the great trees. The guest chambers, the verandahs, the partitions, and the mats, are kept in a state of dazzling cleanliness. The whole establishment is distinguished by elegance and simplicity. Historical remembrances attach to many places in the neighborhood.

A hunting lodge of the *shōgun* formerly occupied the summit of one of the hills, which commands an extensive view of the plains watered by the Sumida-*gawa*. In a narrow valley, at some distance, is pointed out a temple consecrated to Ieyasu, who was its founder, also a miraculous spring which falls from an elevated wall of rocks. This spring is placed under the invocation of a stone idol, to which the frequenters of the gardens address their prayers. Heated by the fumes of *sake*, they place themselves under the falling water and enjoy the natural bath. In the little hamlets of the plain a quantity of shops or booths offer all sorts of curiosities and trinkets to the choice of the visitors and their children. A lively trade is done by these traders, for no family ever returns from a party in the country without bringing home some remembrance of the village markets.

The real secret of the celebrity of the gardens of Ōji is, that they were placed in very ancient times under the patronage of Inari, the tutelary god of the rice fields, and conjointly under the protection of the sacred animal that is his attribute, that is to say, *kitsune*, the fox, who deigns to honor the country with his particular favor. He is worshipped on the hill bearing the name of Ōji Inari.

On the seventeenth day of the first month an innumerable crowd of citizens and country people flock to his temple. They hang up ex-votos, and deposit their new year's tribute in the money box. Then the crowd disperses, wandering in groups through the groves, and contemplate from afar a great tree in the marsh, around which an annual sabbat of the foxes has been held on the previous night. Persons who pretend to have seen the assembly of the foxes preceded by a will-o'-the-wisp and followed by the spirits of the rice fields, are eagerly interrogated, and bear their testimony gravely to the character of the festival, the number of the foxes, and the gaiety manifested on the occasion.

These particulars having been ascertained, inferences are drawn from them respecting the year that is commencing, and the abundance and the quality of the harvest are prognosticated. Then the visitors, seat themselves around the *hibachi* in the guest chambers of the teahouse, and talk in a low voice of the mysterious influence of *kitsune* in the affairs of this world. What is chance? what is hazard? good or bad fortune?—words devoid of sense. Still, there is something behind these words, because every time one uses them one is forced to it by circumstances. The fox has come that way. "I," says one of the guests, "have had the misfortune to lose a child, the doctor could not even tell me the seat of his malady." While the mother was grieving, the lamps, which were placed beside the corpse, threw the shadow of the poor woman on the opposite wall, everyone in the chamber of mourning perceived at once that the shadow had taken the form of a fox. "And travellers," continues a neighbor, "when they see their road prolonging itself indefinitely, although they have calculated the distance, is it not because they have omitted to count with the tail of the fox? How many times have they not wandered about the rice fields, misguided by the will-o'-the-wisp, which *kitsune* can make to flicker where he chooses. And the hunters—how many tricks has he not played on them? If a good sportsman was to dare to attempt to revenge himself, he would only have the mortification of seeing the fox bounding and jumping before him, and carrying away in his mouth the arrow that had been let fly at him."

The annals of Japan state that *kitsune* is capable of metamorphosis. When Emperor Konoe, who reigned in 1150, found himself under the painful necessity of dismissing his favorite, Tamamo no Mae, in order to save the finances of the empire from complete ruin, the fair one escaped from her apartments in the farm of a white fox adorned with six fan-shaped tails. Cases no less extraordinary are quoted of the abduction of young girls, some of whom have never returned, while others on their return have closed their parents' mouths by the word *kitsune*!

When it pleases the latter to disguise himself as an old monk, he is most dangerous. There is always one means of defeating him. *Kitsune*, whatever may be his disguise, never resists the suggestions of his nose. Let anyone place a rat newly roasted in the path of the false priest, and he will not fail to forget his personation, and fall on the prey, forgetful of everything else.

The *yamabushi*, or ascetic hermits of the mountains, generally succeed in keeping *kitsune* at a distance, because they know how to practise on his weakness. But they also must be particularly on their guard to avoid a surprise. If the fox succeeds in discovering their barrel of *sake*, woe to them who shall taste it afterwards! It is thus that some very respectable *yamabushi* have become objects of popular derision. A few cups suffice to turn their heads, they throw off their clothing, utter cries, gesticulate like madmen, and execute the most eccentric dances, also danced by two foxes in the same step, who mark the time, one by blowing a sacred conch, the other by flourishing about the holy water brush of the poor bewitched monks. It is also said that the peasants, whenever they have slept in the rice fields, are liable to be caught in the nooses of *kitsune*, who deprives them, according to his fancy, of the use of their limbs or the freedom of movement.

The Japanese people have also their romance of the fox. They amuse themselves with their hero, though they are afraid of him. The *kitsune* becomes in turn a sacred, amusing, perfidious, and diabolical personage. In the morning they pay him homage, in the evening they turn him into ridicule. But if he lends himself to jesting, it is only to take a more signal revenge. Let anyone try, for example, in family festivals or in social banquets, to amuse themselves at the expense of *kitsune* and to try his patience, when he shall have joined the party in earnest, he will then soon turn all their heads the wrong way, and the night will not pass without his strewing the ground with those who have given him provocation. The game of the fox begins, very innocently in appearance, with a kind of song and clapping of hands. Three attitudes are taken alternately. The first consists in raising the hands, and holding them half shut behind the ears, the second, in doubling the fist and stretching out the forearm, the third, of opening both hands and spreading them on the knees. This is called the game of the fox, the gun, and the *yakunin*. The fox loses against the gun, because the gun kills, the gun loses against the *yakunin*, because the *yakunin* can defend himself, finally, the *yakunin* loses against the fox, because *kitsune* is the most cunning animal in creation. The losing party is compelled to drink a cup of *sake*.

It is easy to conceive that under the influence of such a penalty the game becomes more and more animated. Some of the players find it too sedentary, one of them rises, and, amid the acclamations of the company, procures a long rope, makes a running knot, holds it by one end, and throws the other to a companion, who stretches the rope as tight as he can without spoiling the running knot. Behind the latter is placed a little stand, on which lies what is called the rat—it is a cap or cup, or any other object—which the fox must take away quickly, without letting himself be caught in the noose. If the guardians of the rat pull the cord between their hands too quickly or too slowly, they pay the penalty. If the fox be caught, were it only by the end of the finger, he has to defray the expense of any amount of drinks so long as it pleases the guests of both sexes who enjoy the spectacle of his captivity. In such cases, the ordinary resources of the orchestra fail to express the delight of the company. The guests knock their glasses or porcelain cups together like bells, the singers imitate the cries of all sorts of animals, the more active hop round the unfortunate fox, and mock him with every kind of grimace. *Kitsune* of the mountains, from his hiding place, contemplates all the details of this Bacchic scene, and thrills with pleasure when it attains its height.

Better than this foolish amusement are the quiet picnics that take place in the suburbs during the fine season. Two or three families arrange to pass an evening together in the country, either on the shady hills overlooking the bay, or in the great orchards on the north side, from where a full view of Fuji-*yama* may be had. They are preceded by attendants, who, on reaching the place agreed on, trace out a reserved space by means of long pieces of material stretched on poles. Within this they lay down mats. Stoves are prepared, with kettles for making tea, and pans for frying fish. The company arrive and install themselves, the ladies unpacking the provisions, and the festival begins. It lasts until sunset, games, singing, and music, animating the scene. Sometimes professional singers are summoned to the festival, and occasionally even a couple of wandering dancers, whose speciality consists of pantomime, posturing, and character figures. One of their prettiest performances is called the fan-dance, it is a kind of pantomime, generally executed by a young girl in the costume of a page. There are also some national dances kept up in the society of the town, and these naturally have a place among the diversions of the country parties. Generally, ladies dance alone, they form a quadrille, and the dance consists principally of gestures, without any change of position, except in passing from one attitude to another. They stretch out their hands and arms, sometimes the right, and sometimes the left, not without grace or elegance, but the movement is exceedingly monotonous. A man never dances, except when, inspired by the fumes of *sake*, he imitates some choreographic feat which he has witnessed on the stage.

But, as I have already said, it is not only pleasure that attracts the citizens to the groves of the outer suburbs. He loves the place for its own sake, he knows it under all aspects and in all seasons, he knows its curiosities and peculiarities, its local kermesses, its annual markets, at which he purchases a part of his household provisions. He goes to the public auctions of rice, vegetables, fruits, and coal, which take place at fixed periods in certain rural districts. He also goes to see the antique cedar on which he has painted the initials of his name and the date of his first visit. And he knows one still more ancient, which contains a natural reservoir of water celebrated for its efficacy against certain diseases. This tree was planted by a *kami*.

For a few centimes he is permitted to fish in the tanks of the monastery, and to carry home the results of his sport. There is not a convent, or temple, or shrine in the neighborhood which is not distinguished by some more or less interesting peculiarity. Here a group of palm trees, there bananas and bamboos, or evergreen oaks, or maples, or gigantic azaleas. And the monastic orders to which the convents belong devote themselves to the education of tortoises and mandarin ducks, or to making sweetmeats.

Many of the hills have a special reputation, this one because it affords the best open-air view of the princely spectacle of hawking, that one because it overlooks a famous battlefield. Several are covered with tombs, ranged in terraces like little gardens. The monuments present an infinite variety of style of ornamentation according to the social condition and sect of the deceased, most frequently a tablet bearing an epitaph rests on the shell of a large stone tortoise, the symbol of eternity. A great number of tombs are formed of a socket surmounted by a statue of Buddha, or some auxiliary divinity of Buddhism, such as Kannon or Amida, standing on a lotus flower. These images are cut in granite, or basalt, in extremely fine workmanship. The most ancient are moss-grown, or smothered in branches of ivy and other climbing plants. Gigantic pines, cypress trees, and laurels, lend a charm by their picturesque grouping to the burial places.

One of the most interesting cemeteries in the neighborhood of Edo is that of the Shōrin-*ji* cemetery, it is specially reserved for men illustrious in letters or sciences.

At the entrance of the villages, and sometimes in the open country, we find stones erected to commemorate some historical event. And frequently little shrines built in honor of some hero who fought in the wars that founded the dynasty of Ieyasu. Buddhism has affixed its stamp to every place worthy of exciting the attention of travellers. There is no grotto without its idol and its story, there is no lake that does not contain a little islet with its temple dedicated to Benten.

It is fortunate for the Japanese that their popular superstitions have developed in them a love of country life, and a proper regard for the vegetable wealth in which their country abounds.

Winds of Change

The bombardment of Kagoshima, and the destruction of the batteries at Shimonoseki, were, in reality, only incidents in the question of the external relations inaugurated by the treaties. It was, however, difficult to avoid connecting them with the internal political question that was agitating the privileged classes of the empire.

These events were apparently of a nature to confirm the previsions respecting the future of Japan which had long been cherished in secret. The country, hitherto so deeply divided, was about to reconstitute itself on a fresh basis. It aspired to order, to unity, to political centralization. What was there to prevent its attainment of them? Just two things, which the government might easily realize with the moral support of the oowers interested in its preservation. The first was the definitive subjection of the feudal nobility to the civil and political power concentrated in the *shōgun*, the second was the complete emancipation of the Bakufu from the supremacy of the emperor in everything concerning temporal affairs. The successors of Ieyasu regarded the latter point as settled, as an acquired right, so decidedly, that the court of Edo considered it highly improper and unconstitutional that the legations should have demanded from the emperor the ratification of the treaties concluded by the *shōgun* in all the plenitude of his legal competence. At the rate at which events were succeeding each other in Japan, the double solution, which was to secure the unification and the peace of the empire and to consolidate its commercial relations with the West, was advancing with rapid strides. The rising of the *daimyō* of the south against the *shōgun*, and the succession to the throne of a man of the capacity of Tokugawa Yoshinobu, would no doubt precipitate the denouement, the issue could not be doubtful.

Europeans inevitably commit the error of transacting their affairs in the Eastern world in too systematic a spirit. In this particular case, England, happily guided by the instinct of commercial interests, made an exception to this rule. She became the friend and confidant of the *daimyō* whose capital she had shortly before burned to ashes. The insurrection of the *daimyō* of the south speedily assumed threatening proportions. In place of opposing to it the resistance that had been expected from his energy, and from the considerable military preparations he had made with the assistance of France, Yoshinobu suddenly abdicated, "through patriotism," according to the version of the Tokugawa. He begged the emperor to convoke all the great men of the empire, in order to establish the government on a solid basis, to revise the constitution, and thus to open up for the country a path of progress that should lead it to power and prosperity.

The emperor complied with Yoshinobu's request. But the assembly of *daimyō* was tumultuous, and ended by a sort of *coup d'etat* on the part of the confederates of the south. They carried the emperor and his court forcibly into their camp, dispersed the friends of the *shōgun*, and promulgated decrees abolishing the Bakufu and placing executive power in the hands of the emperor. But then Yoshinobu made up his mind to open the campaign. The four *yashiki* Satsuma possessed at Edo, and served as a centre of operations for the conspirators in the capital, were attacked and destroyed by cannon. The preceding *shōgun* had previously demolished the residence of Nagato in order to disprove his connivance in the aggressions of that *daimyō* on the Europeans. The army of Yoshinobu formed in line at Fushimi, on the north-west of Osaka. The troops of Satsuma, of Chōshū (Nagato), of Tosa, of Awa, of Aki, and others, occupied Kyoto.

The first engagement took place January 28th, 1868. Yoshinobu remained in observation at Osaka. His forces being ill directed, Yoshinobu fell back on the fortress of Edo. On the following days they lost it, retook it, and were finally beaten in a pitched battle, when a great number of his men passed over to the enemy, on the pretext that the latter, having hoisted the standard of the emperor, any further struggle would have been sacrilege. The citadel of Osaka fell, without the firing of a shot, into the hands of the conquerors of Edo, who burned it to ashes. Yoshinobu fled by sea.[1]

The troops of the confederates boldly pushed their advantage, and marched on Edo. But after the *daimyō* of Aizu had obtained some successes over them, an arrangement was come to between the moderates of both camps. Aizu, Sendai, Shōnai, Nagaoka and Yonesawa, made submission. Yoshinobu, who was invited to resume his functions, refused. And a child of six years old, a member of the clan of the Tokugawa, was elected in his stead. As the child's father did not give his assent to this transaction, the emperor pronounced the definitive suppression of the office. He made a solemn entry into Edo on the 25th November, 1868. The citadel was delivered up to him by the *daimyō* of Owari, who belonged to the camp of the confederates. The branch of the *daimyō* of Kyushu played no ostensible part in these troubles.

The Bakufu went down before the first onslaught, under the reign of a *daimyō* of the branch of Mito, and we must seek the cause of this defeat in the bloody rivalry among families that has exhausted the Tokugawa dynasty.

It cannot be said that the pacification of Japan is complete. The last partisans of the north have succumbed after heroic struggles in the island of Hokkaido, of which they had taken possession under the leadership of the gallant young Enomoto Takeaki, admiral of the shogunal fleet. Nevertheless the two parties arc still in an attitude of mutual observation, and their forces remain almost equal. The traditional antipathy that reigns between the *daimyō* of the south and the north is an obstacle to the complete centralization of the administration. A proposal made by Satsuma, that all the *daimyō* of Japan should make a return of their fiefs to the emperor, served only to compromise that *daimyō* in the eyes of his own allies. The emperor's government has recognized the necessity of raising Edo officially to the rank of a second capital of the empire.

The emperor himself cannot do otherwise, in the interest of his relations with the representatives of foreign powers, than reside there for at least a portion of the year. But, in addition to this, there is already a question of

1 Eescorted by the *daimyō* of Aizu and Kuwana, Yoshinobu escaped from Osaka Castle to return to Edo on the shogunal warship *Kaiyō-maru*. As the vessel had not yet arrived, he took refuge for the night on the American warship *USS Iroquois*, anchored in Osaka Bay. The *Kaiyō-maru* arrived two hours later and picked up the Tokugawa party.

the nomination of a viceroy, in order that each of the two capitals may have its court as well as its share of influence in the affairs of state. This would be the re-establishment of the Bakufu under another name, and probably the restoration of the Tokugawa dynasty.

In any case, the fair days of the old regime are past, in the realm of the *daimyō*, and for the gentlemen of Kyoto in general. They must resign themselves to exchange cock-fighting and tennis playing for the burden of public business, and to a daily contact with the Western world. The civil war produced extreme perturbation in the finances of the *daimyō* and the government. The emperor was forced to create paper money, and to give it a forced currency, while refusing to accept it at the public treasury. Commerce complains, according to its right and its duty. But I presume its lamentations are accompanied by a slight smile, and a tolerably clear notion that, in a very short time, dating from the day on which this economic measure shall have fallen into complete discredit, the Japanese will have begun to open the almost virgin mines in which the country abounds, and to hand over the concession and the working of them to the industry of Europeans. Thus, everything is coming to the assistance of the latter, even including those events that are apparently most injurious to the interests of commerce. In fact it is very natural that as breach after breach is made in the old walls of the Japanese edifice, the place should speedily fall into the power of the invaders.

But we must not indulge in illusions with respect to our advantages. It is not our political prestige, nor the splendor of our embassies, that constitute the strongest argument with the Japanese, it is simply the superiority of our civilization from the point of view of the ceramic and industrial arts.

The Japanese are much better informed than we suppose on the general situation in Europe, and the resources of the various states. Their embassies to Europe, between 1860 and 1868, to England, Holland, France, Belgium, Germany, Russia, Switzerland, and Italy, the share in the Paris Universal Exhibition taken by the *shōgun*, the *daimyō* of Satsuma, the *daimyō* of Hizen, and the commerce of Edo. And the studies made in Europe by a relatively considerable number of young Japanese, a contingent which is renewed year after year, have all tended to consolidate the work of the treaties, and secure our improved relations from all the vicissitudes of politics.

Japan has fallen to the West. Since the expeditions of Toyotomi Hideyoshi in Korea, when the troops beat the Chinese auxiliaries despatched to the aid of that kingdom, the government of China has been estranged from Japan. It seems that it has even forbidden its subjects to entertain commercial relations with that country, for the junks that visit Nagasaki and the ports of the inland sea come exclusively from Japan, and belong to a trading corporation that is barely tolerated by the governors of Chekiang.

Of all the countries of the far East, Japan, that is to say, the south of Japan—Shikoku and Kyushu—is most convenient and agreeable to Europeans. The four seasons are very distinctly marked there, from March to the latter half of May, a splendid spring, from June to September, summer, commencing with a brief rainy season, followed by heat, during which the thermometer marks from 63° to 70° Fahrenheit, from September to the end of November is autumn, without great heat, and free from rain, storm, and mosquitoes, finally, three months of winter usually free from tempests, and under a perfectly serene sky, with a temperature that sometimes falls at Yokohama as low as 43° Fahrenheit. From September to April the predominant winds are north and cast, and the rest of the year south and west.

Earthquakes, though frequent, are rarely disastrous, and are generally less dreaded than fires. The latter scourge furnishes one of the most picturesque spectacles of Japanese life. I have frequently been struck, during the conflagrations I have witnessed, by the attitude of the squadrons in the offing, in which the glare of the flames is reflected, the vessels answering, one after another, by luminous signals, to the orders of the admiral. And the men lending their perfectly disciplined aid, in total silence, in the midst of the confusion of the natives. In a short time, the advance of civilization will have considerably reduced danger from fire in Japan. Excellent health may be maintained by combining certain European improvements with the ordinary diet of the Japanese, Tropical fevers are unknown in Japan. And there is less danger to foreigners from cholera, dysentery, and small-pox, all much dreaded by natives, than in Europe.

But the great attraction of Japan is that the commercial preponderance is not so crushing there as in China and the East Indies. On this subject I can amply confirm the judicious and practically interesting observations of

Jaques Siegfried of Mulhause, who says, in his work entitled *Seize Mois au Tour du Monde*:

> The commerce of the East is becoming more and more democratic, each one may take his little share in it. And the door is now open to all the world. The Germans and the Swiss have profited largely by this state of things. They are not content to occupy themselves with the affairs, relatively small, but of still increasing importance, of their own respective countries. Bhut they have mixed themselves up more and more in the commerce of the English, and have succeeded in establishing a formidable competition with them on their own ground, and one which increases daily. The commercial relations of Europe with Japan are doubtless very far from having such importance as those with China and the Indies. The Chinese, Indian, and Japanese trade with Europe and its colonies amounted in 1867, including both exports and imports, to three and a half milliards of francs, which was more than double the amount of ten years before.
>
> The private business done at the principal Japanese port, Yokohama, has also doubled in less than ten years. It may be estimated at 100 millions of francs. This is little. But it is also much, if we take into account the abnormal and unfavorable circumstances of our early relations with Japan. When we look at the proportions between the 30 or 34 millions of Japanese, the 200 millions of Indians, and the 300 or 400 millions of Chinese, there is room, not only for satisfaction with, but also for astonishment at, the considerable progress which we have made in the brief space of ten years. Of all Oriental races, the Japanese accustom themselves most rapidly to our civilization and its necessities, and most readily acquire a taste for the products of our industry. In Japan, therefore, European commerce finds most encouraging elements.

Two principal articles form the basis of the normal commerce of Japan, as regards exportation. They are raw silk and tea. And notwithstanding inevitable fluctuations, the importance of these products cannot do otherwise than augment year by year.

The export of silk from Japan to Europe is estimated at 15,000 bales per annum, and it sends to America alone from 10 to 11 millions of pounds of tea. Japanese tea has not yet found favor in Europe, but I am convinced that, sooner or later, it will be highly appreciated there for its hygienic qualities. The exports of secondary value, but in the category of regular commerce, are vegetable wax, camphor, nutgalls, and soy sauce. Kaw cotton, destined for the Chinese market, copper, highly esteemed in European industries, and coal, which is still very imperfectly worked, are only occasionally objects of any considerable operations.

The trade in silkworms' eggs, being due to accidental causes, cannot be included in the number of the permanent commercial resources of Japan. It has given rise during the last seven years to some considerable transactions. But it is becoming more and more spoiled in the hands of speculators. So long as Japan does not employ machinery in weaving her silks, Europe will be able to utilize her waste as she does at present.

The other Japanese products available for occasional transactions of a very limited kind, are tobacco, flax, ginseng root, fish oil, turnip oil and seed, colza, linseed, twine, brocades, crapes, pierced cocoons, mushrooms, mats, deerhorns, paper—of which there are seventy kinds, ranging from the finest tissue paper to wrappers as thick and as strong as our waxed canvas—lacquer, and other art objects, vitriol, alum, saltpeter, and sulphur. The latter article may sooner or later rival Sicilian sulphur in the American market. To complete this enumeration I must mention the trade solely intended for the Chinese market. The Japanese export to China iron bars of native manufacture, algae—which are much prized for their saline properties in those Chinese provinces in which salt is scarce—chestnuts, potatoes, the pulp of fruits, dried oysters, shrimps, sharks' fins, and timber for building.

The import trade rests, like the export trade, on two capital articles alone, cotton—spun, woven, and printed. And certain woollen materials, or woollen and cotton mixed, which it would be wearisome to enumerate.

The sums the annual export of these manufactures bring to us are far from replacing those expended in our purchases of Japanese rice and teas. Up to the present exceptional circumstances have enabled us to strike the balance between the exportations and the importations, and we may hope that this unforeseen advantage will not fail us for a long time to come.

After the negotiations concerning exchange had been effected, we received commissions for ships of war, armed steamers, batteries of rifled cannon, breech loaders, and ammunition of all kinds, which the Japanese needed for the prosecution of their civil war. We even built a military port for them with docks and a marine arsenal, at Yokosuke, south of Yokohama. They will soon be asking us to work their mines, to establish their telegraphic communication, and to make their railroads. Afterwards the time will come when their windows will be made of glass, instead of slides of transparent paper, when they must have curtains to their windows and mirrors in their drawing rooms, when they will burn gas instead of smoky candles. And when Parisian millinery will have its establishments at Japan, for the Japanese men are already adopting European attire, and we cannot suppose that the women will not follow the fashion.

In the meantime, imports of the second class are limited to the following articles, and in small numbers, lead, tin, tin and zinc in sheets, wire and pewter, watches, articles de Paris, counterpanes, leather, hides, ivory, rhinoceros horns, and sugar.

Besides these, there is a special import trade in supplies for the strangers' quarter, window glass, furniture, pottery, glass, clothes, wine, spirits, and preserved meats. Far from having exaggerated the commercial importance of Japan, I may add, that from this point of view Japan will not for a long time yet give us as much as we might expect. The country is only emerging from a state of things under which it had no consumers outside its own population. The northern portions of the archipelago are generally untilled, and even in the south of Japan there are thousands of uncleared acres, covered with bush and scrub, or turned into parks and unproductive gardens, the mortmain properties of feudal lords and monastic confraternities. Nevertheless, though all this should be utilized, planted with mulberry and camphor, with tea and cotton trees, the smallness of its territory must always prevent Japan from competing in commercial value with countries of such colossal dimensions as China and India.

We must also bear in mind that, in our day, neither the exploitation of textile fabrics, nor that of alimentary products, is the monopoly of any people in particular. Competition in this kind of supply makes giant strides, for the greater good of humanity. Cotton from India has made a place for itself in our markets beside cotton from America, and the Suez Canal will soon be bringing us cotton from the newly-explored regions of Africa. Ten years ago, Europe depended wholly on the Chinese market for tea and for silk. She now has two rival markets at her disposition—China and Japan. Soon perhaps there will exist a third—the Californian, for European speculators are already planting the mulberry, and introducing the culture of silkworms into California, with the assistance of Japanese colonists.

Agriculture is at the basis of all societies, but they grow great only by the arts, or by commerce. Better still, by the constant simultaneous development of those three branches of human activity.

The foundation of social order among the Japanese, as among the Chinese, is agriculture, which both have pushed to the highest point of perfection. It may be said, generally, that the Japanese possess the mercantile faculty in only a slight degree, and that they show a great natural disposition for the arts and for industry. The Chinese, on the contrary, satisfied with their traditional technical processes, and indifferent to all progress, excel in banking as in usury, in high commerce as in the smallest traffic. Let us then leave trade to the Chinese, and give to the Japanese industry.

Mulhause has called them, not without reason, "The French of the East." It behoves them, henceforth, to develop, side by side with their amiable qualities, those of which manufacturers, mechanicians, and magistrates are made. The introduction of the mechanical arts within the tropical zone is, if not impossible, at least devoid of any chance of being made remunerative. China, in so far as she is concerned, rejects every innovation of this kind. Japan, by its geographical position, by the wealth of its soil in coal and metals, by the conditions of its climate and the genius of its people, seems destined to become the central seat of the manufactures, the works, the industry, and the navigation of the whole western basin of the Pacific.

Reform

A brief account of the latest events in Japan is necessary to the completeness of the record contained in the preceding pages.

The patriotic act of the *daimyō* after the downfall of the *shōgun*, and the recovery of executive power by the lawful emperor, formed a striking conclusion to the revolutionary drama. These powerful and semi-independent feudal nobles agreed voluntarily to resign their heritages into the hands of the emperor, and to receive about one-tenth of their former incomes as sufficient to keep up their diminished status. This extraordinary movement was expressed by statesman Akizuki Tanetatsu, in a memorial addressed to the nobles, which ran as follows:

> Let those who wish to show their faith and loyalty act in the following manner, so that they may firmly establish the foundations of the imperial government:
> 1. Let them restore the territories they have received from the emperor, and return to a constitutional and undivided country.
> 2. Let them abandon their titles, and under the name of *kazoku* (noblemen) receive such small properties as may suffice for their wants.
> 3. Let the officers of the clans, abandoning that title, call themselves officers of the emperor, receiving property equal to that which they have hitherto held.
> Let these three important measures be adopted forthwith, in order that the empire may be built up on an imperishable basis.

The whole body of *daimyō*, two hundred and sixty-four in number, gradually gave their support to this scheme of patriotic sacrifice, their fiefs were given up to the emperor, and their extensive domains became subject to taxation by the imperial government. As the right to maintain large bodies of armed retainers was also relinquished, the vast revenues they formerly drew from their territories were no longer necessary.

The revolution being so far accomplished, and political unity and administrational centralization attained, the emperor and his advisers proceeded with rapid strides to the completion of the work of reform. Edict after edict issued from the imperial palace. Edo was to be styled henceforward the capital, "the eastern capital," and to become the seat of government, with Edo castle as the place of the imperial court. Contracts were entered into for constructing a grand trunk railway to connect Edo and Yokohama with Kyoto, Osaka, and Kobe, and for laying a line of telegraph from one end to the other of the empire—between Nagasaki and Edo.

Promising Japanese youths were sent forth by hundreds to Europe and the United States to study the language, laws, literature, and science of those natives of the West who had produced the mental ferment that had led to such great changes. Among the students were many belonging to the highest families, such as Prince Higashifushimi Yorihiro, who came to England, and Prince Kitashirakawa Yoshihisa, who went to Germany, both uncles of the present emperor, his majesty also applied himself diligently to the study of English. Colleges and schools for acquiring all branches of Western knowledge were established in various cities of Japan, and professors invited from Europe and America to fill the posts of instructors. Schools for popular education were formed throughout the empire. The Christian religion was officially tolerated. And further, the calendar of the Christian nations (new style) adopted. To effect this change, the third of the twelfth month of the fifth year of Meiji was made to correspond with the 1st of January 1873. The year was to consist of three hundred and sixty-five days, which were to be divided into twelve months. The 25th of December was to be celebrated as a holiday, not for the same reasons as the Christmas Day of the Christian world, but in honor of the founder of the imperial dynasty, Emperor Jinmu. Each day was to be divided into twenty-four hours, and not into twelve watches, as before. And every seventh day was to be kept as a holiday. Other edicts were directed against ancient customs and habits, ordering this and forbidding that, all with a view to assimilating the life and habits of the people to those of the nations of the Western world.

Amongst the important reforms are those connected with religion. Buddhism has been discouraged, the revenues of many of the temples have been appropriated to imperial purposes, and the priests are being compelled to realize as much of their moveable property as possible, selling their bells and bronze images and ornaments to so great an extent, that the metal has been lately one of the most considerable articles of export from the Japanese ports. Houses for the poor have been established, with the aim of doing away with the numerous beggars in the streets and roads. The great popular festivals and fairs—the *matsuri*—in which this excitable and joyous people took so much delight, have been forbidden, or at least greatly reduced in number. The two-sworded gentry have been abolished, and measures adopted to induce the dangerous *samurai*, or military class, to adopt the safer pursuits of commerce or the civil professions. One of the few changes regretted by those who watch the astonishing transformations so rapidly taking place, is that of the easy and graceful native costumes, which are giving way in most of the chief centers of population, but chiefly in the male sex, to the conventional dress of London and Paris.

In 1872 the first railway in Japan was opened, with imposing ceremony and amid cheering prognostications. It was the first completed section of the trunk line which is to connect the great cities, and extends from Yokohama to Edo, but at present consisting only of a single line of rails. The emperor, throwing aside the traditional mystery that for ages had surrounded the sacred person of the monarch, resolved to open the railway in person, and show himself publicly to the people. A vast concourse of people assembled on the 14th of October at the Edo terminus, and the day was observed as a national holiday. Accommodation was provided for 10,000 persons on the platform, and the emperor desired that all who wished to see the procession announced in the programme for the day should find admittance. The imperial pleasure gardens, formerly the private grounds of the *shōgun*, were thrown open to the public. All the foreign ministers from Yokohama were present, and the representatives of the press invited to attend, in accordance with the most advanced views of modern enlight-enment. At nine in the morning the emperor left the castle, in a state carriage of European construction, and attended by a prince of the imperial family, the prime minister, and a squadron of cavalry, followed by the other members of the Japanese government and by some of the chief nobles then resident in the capital.

Arriving at the station, where he was received by the minister of public works, the chief commissioners of railways, the foreign ministers and other officials, he inspected a plan of the railway. And a procession was then formed to the platform, from which he entered the train, followed by the rest of his suite and the privileged few who were invited to make the journey. On arriving at Yokohama he was received by the governor of Kanagawa, the railway officials, and the consuls of the treaty powers. And, in reply to addresses presented on the part of the foreign residents, delivered the following speech through his minister for foreign affairs:

> I am profoundly pleased to hear the congratulatory words that have been addressed to me by the foreign guests residing at Yokohama. Of the people who live in this country, whether born on the soil or merely temporarily residing here—whether here by chance or voyaging of their own accord—none are deprived of protection or their rights. This work will be still further extended, with the object of increasing our prosperity and of advancing my country on the path of civilization. As long as the harmonious relations now existing between this and foreign countries continue to prevail, I shall have both foreign and native people close to my heart.

The strong feeling of loyalty and veneration entertained by the Japanese for the representative of their ancient line of monarchs, a sentiment that has contributed so much to the success of the late revolution and the overthrow of the usurping Bakufu, was strikingly shown on the departure of the emperor from Yokohama. As soon as he left the pavilion the crowd rushed forward, and, seizing the chair of state and the carpet on which the sacred foot had trod, tore them both to shreds, each possessor of a scrap glorying in his prize. The police were powerless, the crowd was so immense, and their eagerness so uncontrollable, although full of good humor, that it was quite impossible to check them. On his return to Edo the emperor thanked the railway officials, and in another brief speech repeated his intention to develop still further the railway system, until it extended throughout the country. The remainder of the day was spent in joyous festivities, and at night Edo and Yokohama were illuminated.

The spectacle of a great and gifted nation, so long kept in jealous exclusion from the rest of the world, thus emancipating itself from the trammels of a narrow Eastern policy and entering into sympathy with Western civilization, excites the deep interest of moralists and statesmen. It is naturally asked, *Will the change be lasting? Is not the pace too fast, and will not the conservative principle in daimyō and people, at present stunned by the suddenness of the movement, re-assert itself in a disastrous reaction?* Some of the reforms suggested by the more excited partisans of change quite take away one's breath. But they have not at present been adopted. One was a proposition made by Mori Arinori, recently Japanese minister at Washington, for the adoption of the English language in Japan. This would be a clenching method of solving the enormous difficulties in the way of free intercourse presented by the Japanese language. The difficulties lie, however, chiefly in the abstruseness and complication of the written and printed characters, and is partly met by the adoption of the Roman letters and syllabic forms, which are being tried by native scholars and printers.

The fears of a reaction, entertained in Europe and by the foreign mercantile community in Japan, have been to some degree stimulated by the most recent occurrences. During the summer of the present year, serious riots broke out at several places in the interior, the most important of which was at Fukuoka and the adjoining districts, about 150 miles from Nagasaki. Alarming rumors reached the foreign residents, and were transmitted to Europe and America. It was said that the discontented peasantry and farmers had risen to the number of 80,000 men, that the regular army had been defeated and the government stations pillaged and burnt. Subsequent and more reliable accounts show that the number of the rebels had been exaggerated, although they do not diminish the importance of the revolt, which was a reactionary movement against the reforms of government, which so many observers had expected. The exciting cause was the excessive taxes and imports levied in consequence of the greatly increased public expenditure. All taxes and official salaries under the old system were paid in kind—in rice. And one of the greatest economical difficulties of the new order of things has been connected with the substitution of money payments for the old, no longer practicable, system. The introduction of a uniform scale in a country where a system of land taxation in kind had grown up full of complication, of local diversities of measure, allowances, compensations and so forth, was sure to be productive of local discontent. The attempted enforcement of the new taxation laws appears to have been the sole cause of many of the riots that have taken place. But the Fukuoka revolt, after it had made some progress, revealed a deeper discontent, as shown by the following six concessions demanded by the rebels as a condition of laying down their arms:

1. A return to old *han*, or "lordships," restoring to the *daimyō* their lands and incomes.
2. That the officers of the district shall be appointed from among the inhabitants of the district, and not from a distant one.
3. That the incomes and all property of the *samurai* shall be returned.
4. That the taxes shall be reduced by one half for the space of three years.
5. That the government shall cease cutting down the trees in the surrounding district.
6. That the old Japanese calendar be returned to.

According to the latest news this serious outbreak, like many other minor ones, has been overcome, partly by concessions with regard to taxes and small matters involving no sacrifice of new principles, and partly by the valor and constancy of the native troops. A most encouraging feature of the Fukuoka revolt was the fidelity of the *samurai* to the government, and the aid they lent, as a volunteer force, in the defeat of the rebels.

The present attitude of outside observers with regard to Japan is one of expectancy. The effects of the great political and social changes that have taken place have not yet had time to develop themselves. It is hoped, by all who take an affectionate interest in this singular people, that those effects will not involve the decay of the better traits in their national character. In some respects the recent news from Japan is encouraging, as showing the vigor of the executive and some progress among the people in the assimilation of the new ideas. Evidence of greater caution in the government than was first observed is not wanting, though perhaps the caution may be displaced. Thus, whilst foreigners are clamoring for the right of free access to all parts of the empire, the emperor and his ministers withhold the privilege, or make it known that they will not grant it, except on the condition of the submission of foreign residents to Japanese jurisdiction.

It is the same with regard to the great mineral resources of the country: no facilities are given by law to the working of coal and other mines by foreigners, or to the formation of equitable contracts with foreigners. So strong, in fact, is still the jealousy of foreign participation in the benefits of their country, that it is delaying, by the preference given to inefficient native contractors, the completion of great public works, such as the telegraph line from Nagasaki to Edo.

Commerce, however, is steadily increasing, and a whole fleet of passenger steamers keeps up continual communication between their ports and the great marts of Europe and America. The Japanese have become great travellers and accomplished linguists. To this extent at least the change is beneficent and irrevocable.

Glossary

amado:	Siding shutter.
andon:	Paper-covered lamp stand.
basha:	Carriage.
bessho:	Place (during the Heian and Kamakura periods) where monks withdrew from involvement in temple affairs to devote themselves to religious practice.
danna:	Master, husband, sir.
daimyō:	Feudal lord.
eta:	A caste group whose employment in jobs was considered unclean, setting them apart in medieval society.
fundoshi:	Undergarment for adult males, made from a length of cotton.
furo:	Bath.
fusuma:	Sliding door covered with thick paper.
futon:	Quilted mattress rolled out on the floor for use as a bed.
geisha:	A woman professionally trained to entertain customers with music, dancing, food and drinks, and witty stories.
haori:	Lightweight silk jacket originally meant to be worn by men.
harakiri:	Ritual suicide.
inrō:	A nest of small boxes carried suspended from the belt.
jinrikisha:	Rickshaw.
kago:	Litter.
kakemono:	Hanging scroll.

Bakumatsu Japan

kimono:	Traditional female garment.
kura:	Storehouse.
kuruma:	Vehicle, drawn by either by man or animal.
kurumaya:	Person who draws a kuruma.
netsuke:	Small figure of ivory, wood, metal, or ceramic, used as a buttonlike fixture on a man's sash.
mairimashō:	Let's go.
mikado:	emperor.
nō:	Classical Japanese dance-drama employing highly stylized dances.
o-yu:	Hot water.
rōnin:	Masterless *samurai*.
sake:	Japanese rice wine.
samurai:	Warrior.
sennin:	Immortal, often a hermit living a secluded life among the mountains.
shamisen:	Three-stringed musical instrument.
shide:	Zigzag-shaped paper streamers used in ropes at Shintō shrines or used in Shintō rituals.
shōgun:	hereditary military ruler during Japan's feudal era.
shōji:	Lightweight sliding doors covered with paper.
sōhei:	Warrior-monk.
taikō:	Title given to the regent (*sesshō* or *kanpaku*) on his retirement from office.
tokonoma:	Alcove in which scrolls and ikebana are put on display.
torii:	Gateway commonly built at the entrance to a Shintō shrine.
tōrō:	Lantern.
tsuba:	Sword guard.
yama:	Mountain.
yashiki:	Samurai mansion.
yukata:	Informal light cotton *kimono*.

Index

TOYO REFERENCE SERIES
HEARN'S JAPAN
VOLUME 1
LAFCADIO HEARN
EDITED BY WILLIAM DE LANGE

TOYO REFERENCE SERIES
HEARN'S JAPAN
VOLUME 2
LAFCADIO HEARN
EDITED BY WILLIAM DE LANGE

TOYO REFERENCE SERIES
HEARN'S JAPAN
VOLUME 3
LAFCADIO HEARN
EDITED BY WILLIAM DE LANGE

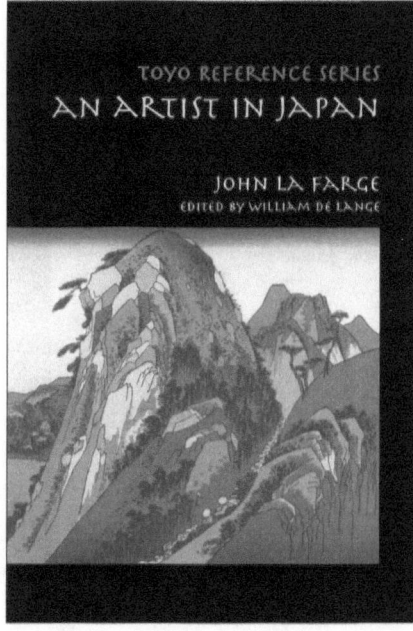

TOYO REFERENCE SERIES
AN ARTIST IN JAPAN
JOHN LA FARGE
EDITED BY WILLIAM DE LANGE

TOYO REFERENCE SERIES
SAMURAI TRAILS

LUCIAN SWIFT KIRTLAND
EDITED BY WILLIAM DE LANGE

TOYO REFERENCE SERIES
TRAVELING JAPAN'S DEEP INTERIOR

ISABELLA LUCY BIRD
EDITED BY WILLIAM DE LANGE

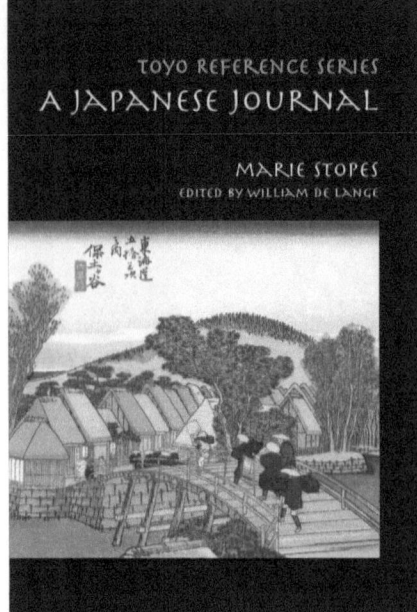

TOYO REFERENCE SERIES
A JAPANESE JOURNAL

MARIE STOPES
EDITED BY WILLIAM DE LANGE

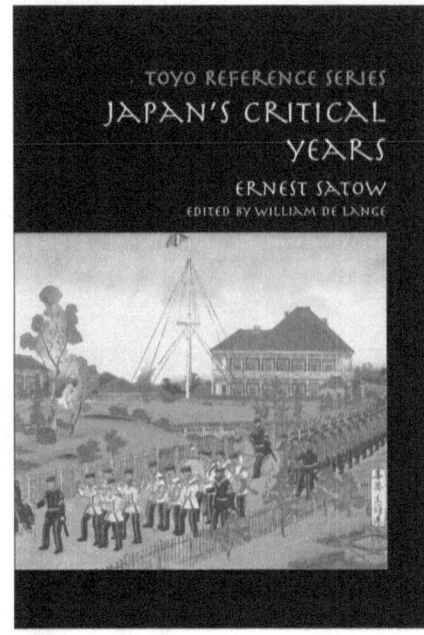

TOYO REFERENCE SERIES
JAPAN'S CRITICAL YEARS

ERNEST SATOW
EDITED BY WILLIAM DE LANGE